ZERO POINT OF JAIN ASTRONOMY

Also by the author:

1. Vedic Physics: Scientific Origin of Hinduism
2. India before Alexander: A New Chronology
3. India after Alexander: The Age of Vikramādityas
4. India after Vikramāditya: The Melting Pot
5. Zero Points of Vedic Astronomy: Discovery of the Original Boundaries of Nakshatras
6. An Alternative Timeline of Indian History: From Buddha and Mahavira to Bappa Rawal

Zero Point of Jain Astronomy

The Origin of Mālava Era

Raja Ram Mohan Roy, Ph.D.

Mount Meru Publishing

Library and Archives Canada Cataloguing in Publication

Title: Zero point of Jain astronomy: the origin of Mālava Era/ Raja Ram Mohan Roy, Ph.D.
Names: Roy, Raja Ram Mohan, 1966- author.
Description: Includes bibliographical references and index.
Identifiers: Canadiana (print) 20190115599 | Canadiana (ebook) 20190115629 | ISBN 9781988207223 (softcover) | ISBN 9781988207216 (ebook)
Subjects: LCSH: Jaina cosmology. | LCSH: Jainism. | LCSH: Astronomy.
Classification: LCC BL1375.C6 R69 2020 | DDC 520—dc23

Published in 2020 by:
Mount Meru publishing
P.O. Box 30026, Cityside Postal Outlet PO
Mississauga, Ontario
Canada L4Z 0B6
Email: mountmerupublishing@gmail.com
Web: https://www.mountmerupublishing.com/
Facebook: https://www.facebook.com/MountMeruPublishing

ISBN 978-1-988207-22-3

Dedicated to
Dr. Manish Mehta and Dr. Sulekh Jain

CONTENTS

FOREWORD

I am delighted to write the foreword for this book on Jain astronomy. I met Dr. Roy first during the biennial JAINA Convention held in July 2017 in Edison, New Jersey and again during the biennial JAINA Convention held in July 2019 in Ontario, California. He made intellectually stimulating presentations on Jain science and astronomy during both conventions. We had extensive discussions on ancient Indian history and science following the presentations. What struck me most during the discussions was Dr. Roy's unique ability to use scientific approach to critically analyze the historical data and point out that the data undeniably supports an alternative timeline of ancient Indian history.

Currently accepted history of India is based on two sheet anchors that connect Indian rulers with European rulers.These two sheet anchors establish that Greek rulers were contemporaries of Mauryan rulers. Dr. Roy has developed an alternative and credible timeline based on Greek rulers being contemporaries of Imperial Gupta rulers. He has come to this conclusion based on in-depth analysis of available data. His work shows that historians have force-fitted the data to the accepted timeline instead of critically analyzing the data. Indian history has been used as a tool to advance the goals of the British Empire and later to advance certain political ideologies. Looking at history from certain self-serving angles has resulted in distorted history which whitewashes the crimes of the invaders and colonizers and undermines the remarkable accomplishments of the native civilization. Historical events showing natives in positive light have been overlooked or misinterpreted. In their zeal to put forward their biased narrative as truth, the chronology of historical events has been pushed forward to give credit to foreigners for certain advances in science and technology, be it mathematics, astronomy, medicines, or metallurgy. Time has come to use science as a tool to do a proper analysis of data so that truth is discovered, and credit could be given to those who deserve it.

In this thoroughly researched scholarly work, archaeoastronomy has been used to determine when and where astronomical observations described in Jain texts were made. It gives an overview of nakṣatra system and describes how the position of sun among the background of stars was changing over time according to Indian texts. Based on this information, the dates of different texts have been determined. In the light of this information, it can be said with confidence that Indian civilization is indigenous, at least starting from Indus Valley Civilization and the evidence incontrovertibly refutes the Aryan Invasion Theory.

In the final analysis, truth is far more important than the dogma often produced by the conventional approaches, and the credence that is driven by the pedigree and position one holds. This choke hold and dominance of some in academia with its biases and speculations has suppressed and/or distorted the truth for far too long. With the arrival of internet age, knowledge has been democratized. It is no longer a fiefdom of those who sit in ivory towers and form mutual admiration clubs. Going forward, history will be better served by those with strong scientific backgrounds, well versed with data analytics, and applying these skills to analyze ancient Indian texts. It is time to pass on the baton to new generation of scholars who can think afresh and discover the true history of India.

I want to congratulate Dr. Raja Ram Mohan Roy for this excellent and well researched book. I sincerely believe that this will set a new yard stick for other scholars in future.

Mukesh Chatter
Concord, MA
May 21st, 2020

PREFACE

I have had great respect for Jainism since childhood. It was out of my reverence for Jainism that I wrote an article titled "Genius of the Jains", which was published by IndiaFacts in March 2017. The article drew the attention of Dr. Manish Mehta, who in consultation with Dr. Sulekh Jain invited me to give two presentations during the biennial JAINA Convention held in July 2017 in Edison, New Jersey. Both of them encouraged me to pursue my interest in Jain astronomy following the convention. The findings of my research in archaeoastronomy carried out since then are being presented in this book and a companion to this book titled "Zero Points of Vedic Astronomy: Discovery of the Original Boundaries of Nakshatras".

I would like to thank Mr. Mithilesh Jha, Mr. Gauri Shankar Jha and Dr. Surjeet Sira for reading the draft and providing comments and suggestions. I would like to give special thanks to Mr. Pankaj Shah for his extensive review of the manuscript. Mr. Mukesh Chettar deserves a very special acknowledgement for his review, support, advice and encouragement. I would also like to thank Dr. Manish Mehta and Dr. Sulekh Jain for their support and encouragement. I would like to express my sincere appreciation to my wife Manju for her continued and enthusiastic support for this work.

Raja Ram Mohan Roy
Mississauga, Canada
October 13, 2020

"The cosmos is all that is or ever was or ever will be."
- Carl Sagan

1. Introduction to Jain Astronomy

Jainism is the most peaceful, tolerant and ecologically friendly religion in the world. Jain texts contain a lot of scientific information that needs to be properly interpreted to understand their significance. A lot of scientific information has been described symbolically for ease of transmission through the ages. Without the proper understanding of the symbolism used by Jain scientists, the ideas propounded in Jain texts will seem difficult to comprehend.

Jain literature is vast, and immense effort has gone into preserving the Jain texts amid the chaos created by the foreign invasions of India. Jain texts are divided in four groups:

1. Prathamānuyoga (preliminary study)
2. Karaṇānuyoga (study of operations) or Gaṇitānuyoga (study of mathematics)
3. Charaṇānuyoga (study of conduct)
4. Dravyānuyoga (study of materials)

Out of these texts, Karaṇānuyoga consists of the following texts:

1. Tiloya Paṇṇatti (Triloka Prajñapti)
2. Trilokasāra
3. Jambudwīpa Prajñapti
4. Sūrya Prajñapti
5. Chandra Prajñapti
6. Lokavibhāga
7. Saṃgaho

The subject of Jain cosmology and astronomy is discussed in detail in these texts belonging to Karaṇānuyoga.

1.1 Jain cosmology

The universe has neither a beginning nor an end in time according to Jain cosmology. The Jain time cycle consists of two halves, Utsarpiṇī and Avasarpiṇī. Each half is further subdivided in six parts. Each part consists of a combination of Suṣamā and Duḥṣamā. Suṣamā denotes happiness and Duḥṣamā denotes unhappiness. Suṣamā Suṣamā denotes extreme happiness, while Duḥṣamā Duḥṣamā denotes extreme unhappiness. The Jain time cycle starts with a period of extreme unhappiness and gradually moves to a period of extreme happiness in the first half. In the second half, it starts with a period of extreme happiness and ends with a period of extreme unhappiness. Jain time cycle was extremely vast and is shown in Table 1.1 [1, 2].

We can see from this table that Jains dealt with numbers that were unbelievably large and no other ancient civilization was equipped to deal with such numbers.

Table 1.1: Jain time cycle

Time unit [1]	Conversion factor [1]	Modern units [2]
1 Nimeṣa	1 Nimeṣa	0.11 seconds
1 Kāṣṭhā	18 Nimeṣa	2 seconds
1 Lava	2 Kāṣṭhā	4 seconds
1 Kalā	2 Lava	8 seconds
1 Leśa	2 Kalā	16 seconds
1 Kṣaṇa	15 Leśa	4 minutes
1 Ghaṭikā	6 Kṣaṇa	24 minutes
1 Muhūrta	2 Ghaṭikā	0.8 hour
1 Divasa	30 Muhūrta	1 day
1 Pakṣa	15 Divasa	15 days
1 Māsa	2 Pakṣa	1 month
1 Ṛtu	2 Māsa	2 months
1 Ayana	3 Ṛtu	6 months
1 Varṣa	2 Ayana	1 year
1 Yuga	5 Varṣa	5 years
1 Śatavarṣa	20 Yuga	100 years
1 Sahasravarṣa	10 Śatavarṣa	1000 years
1 Lākhavarṣa	100 Sahasravarṣa	100,000 years
1 Pūrvāṅga	84 Lākhavarṣa	8.4×10^6 years
1 Pūrva	8.4×10^6 Pūrvāṅga	7.06×10^{13} years
1 Truṭitāṅga	8.4×10^6 Pūrva	5.93×10^{20} years
1 Truṭita	8.4×10^6 Truṭitāṅga	4.98×10^{27} years
1 Aḍaḍāṅga	8.4×10^6 Truṭita	4.18×10^{34} years

Table 1.1: Jain time cycle (continued)

1 Aḍaḍa	8.4 x 10^6 Aḍaḍāṅga	3.51 x 10^{41} years
1 Avavāṅga	8.4 x 10^6 Aḍaḍa	2.95 x 10^{48} years
1 Avava	8.4 x 10^6 Avavāṅga	2.48 x 10^{55} years
1 Huhukāṅga	8.4 x 10^6 Avava	2.08 x 10^{62} years
1 Huhuka	8.4 x 10^6 Huhukāṅga	1.75 x 10^{76} years
1 Utpalāṅga	8.4 x 10^6 Huhuka	1.23 x 10^{83} years
1 Utpala	8.4 x 10^6 Utpalāṅga	1.04 x 10^{90} years
1 Padmāṅga	8.4 x 10^6 Utpala	8.71 x 10^{96} years
1 Padma	8.4 x 10^6 Padmāṅga	7.31 x 10^{103} years
1 Nalināṅga	8.4 x 10^6 Padma	6.14 x 10^{110} years
1 Nalina	8.4 x 10^6 Nalināṅga	5.16 x 10^{117} years
1 Arthanipurāṅga	8.4 x 10^6 Nalina	4.34 x 10^{124} years
1 Arthanipura	8.4 x 10^6 Arthanipurāṅga	3.64 x 10^{131} years
1 Ayutāṅga	8.4 x 10^6 Arthanipura	3.06 x 10^{138} years
1 Ayuta	8.4 x 10^6 Ayutāṅga	2.57 x 10^{145} years
1 Nayutāṅga	8.4 x 10^6 Ayuta	2.16 x 10^{152} years
1 Nayuta	8.4 x 10^6 Nayutāṅga	1.81 x 10^{159} years
1 Prayutāṅga	8.4 x 10^6 Nayuta	1.52 x 10^{166} years
1 Prayuta	8.4 x 10^6 Prayutāṅga	1.28 x 10^{173} years
1 Chūlikāṅga	8.4 x 10^6 Prayuta	1.07 x 10^{180} years
1 Chūlikā	8.4 x 10^6 Chūlikāṅga	9.03 x 10^{186} years
1 Sīrṣa Prahelikāṅga	8.4 x 10^6 Chūlikā	7.58 x 10^{193} years
1 Sīrṣa Prahelikā	8.4 x 10^6 Sīrṣa Prahelikāṅga	6.37 x 10^{200} years

Table 1.1: Jain time cycle (continued)

	1 Sīrṣa Prahelikā	1 numerable year
	1 Palyopama	1 innumerable year
1 Sāgaropama	1 x 10^{15} Palyopama	1 x 10^{15} innumerable years
1 Kālachakra (time cycle)	2 x 10^{15} Sāgaropama	2 x 10^{30} innumerable years

An example of an unimaginably large number in modern mathematics is a Googol, which is equal to 10^{100}. Google is a misspelling of Googol by its founders. The number of years in one Sīrṣa Prahelikā is larger than the square of Googol! Even this number was a small number for Jains, who proposed the unit Palyopama for an innumerable amount of time. They went even beyond this number postulating one quadrillion Palyopama in one Sāgaropama. One time cycle of Jains consisted of two quadrillion Sāgaropama.

Dealing with such immense numbers led Jains to make many important contributions to Mathematics far ahead of their rediscovery in modern times. Important Jain texts detailing mathematical knowledge are Sūrya Prajñapti (4th or 3rd century BCE), Jambudwīpa Prajñapti (4th or 3rd century BCE), Sthānāṅga Sūtra (2nd-1st century BCE), Uttarādhyayana Sūtra (2nd-1st century BCE), Bhagavatī Sūtra (2nd-1st century BCE), and Anuyoga Dvāra Sūtra (2nd-1st century BCE) [3]. The Sthānāṅga Sūtra divides the study of mathematics under ten different sections: parikarma, vyavahāra, rajju, rāśi, kalāsavarṇa, yāvat-tāvat, varga, ghana, varga-varga and vikalpa. Parikarma dealt with simple arithmetic calculations such as addition, subtraction, multiplication and division; vyavahāra with advanced arithmetic; rajju with geometry; rāśi with mensuration; kalāsavarṇa with fractions; yāvat-tāvat with linear equations, varga with quadratic equations; ghana with cubic equations; varga-varga with biquadratic equations; and vikalpa with permutations and combinations [4-5].

Jains divided numbers in three types: enumerable, innumerable and infinite. Anuyoga Dvāra Sūtra describes five types of infinity: infinite in one direction, infinite in two directions, infinite in area, infinite everywhere, and infinite perpetually [4]. The distinction between different types of infinities such as countable infinity (e.g. integers, rational numbers) and uncountable infinity (e.g. real numbers) was proposed by Georg Cantor in 1874 [6]. Jains had proposed similar ideas nearly 2,000 years before Cantor.

Anuyoga Dvāra Sūtra also talks about successive squaring: a^2, $(a^2)^2$, $((a^2)^2)^2$, …; and successive square rooting: $a^{1/2}$, $(a^{1/2})^{1/2}$, $((a^{1/2})^{1/2})^{1/2}$, … . It then gives the following formulas:

$$a^{1/2} \text{ x } a^{1/4} = (a^{1/4})^3$$

$$a^{1/4} \text{ x } a^{1/8} = (a^{1/8})^3$$

$$2^{64} \text{ x } 2^{32} = 2^{96}$$

These calculations led to the independent discovery of logarithms to the bases 2, 3 and 4 as elaborated in Dhavala commentary by Vīrasenāchārya around eighth century CE [4]. Arddhachheda was the term used for logarithm to the base 2, trikachhheda was the term used for logarithm to the base 3 and chaturthachhheda was the term used for logarithm to the base 4. The following formulas were also known:

$$\log_2(m \times n) = \log_2 m + \log_2 n$$
$$\log_2(m \div n) = \log_2 m - \log_2 n$$
$$\log_2 m^n = n \times \log_2 m$$

The concept of logarithm on base 10 was proposed by John Napier in 1614 [7]. Jains had developed the concept of logarithm more than eight centuries before its discovery in the west.

Bhagavatī Sūtra gives the formulas for permutation and combination as follows:

$$_nC_1 = n$$
$$_nC_2 = n \times (n-1)/(1 \times 2)$$
$$_nC_3 = n \times (n-1) \times (n-2)/(1 \times 2 \times 3)$$
$$_nP_1 = n$$
$$_nP_2 = n \times (n-1)$$
$$_nP_3 = n \times (n-1) \times (n-2)$$

It also says that the formulas can be extended to numbers up to infinity. These discoveries predate the development of the theory of permutation by Fabian Stedman in 1677 [8] by over eighteen centuries.

Jain text Triloka Prajñapti written by Yativṛṣabha gives formulas for the first term, common difference, number of terms and sum of terms of an arithmetic progression [4]. This text was written in 500 CE and predates the treatment of arithmetic progression by Carl Friedrich Gauss in late eighteenth century [9] by nearly thirteen centuries.

Jain mathematician Halāyudha wrote a commentary on Piṅgala's Chandaḥsāstra in tenth century CE [4]. He gave a pictorial representation of Meru Prastāra, which is known as Pascal's triangle currently. It is named after Blaise Pascal, who described the binomial coefficients in form of a triangle in 1653 [10]. The formulation by Halāyudha predates the work of Pascal by over six centuries.

Coming back to cosmology, the shape of the universe according to Jain cosmology is shown in Figure 1.1. The base of the universe is 7 Rajju wide. It gradually tapers to 1 Rajju wide in the middle at the height of 7 Rajju. It then increases gradually to 5 Rajju and then tapers back to 1 Rajju at the top. Total height of the universe is 14 Rajju. The depth of the universe is 7 Rajju in the Digambara tradition and thus the volume of the universe in this tradition is 343 cubic Rajju. Depth of the universe changes with height in the Śvetāmbara tradition and the volume of the universe in this tradition is 239 cubic Rajju. Rajju is an extremely large unit of length, whose exact measurement is difficult to establish. The universe has a clear boundary in Jain astronomy and the space inside the universe is called Lokākāśa, while the space outside the universe is called Alokākāśa.

Universe is divided in three main parts. Gods such as Indra live in the upper half called Urdhva Loka or upper world and various types of hell are located in the lower half called Adho Loka or lower world. At the very top of the universe is the abode of liberated beings. Humans and animals live in the middle of the universe called Madhya Loka or middle world.

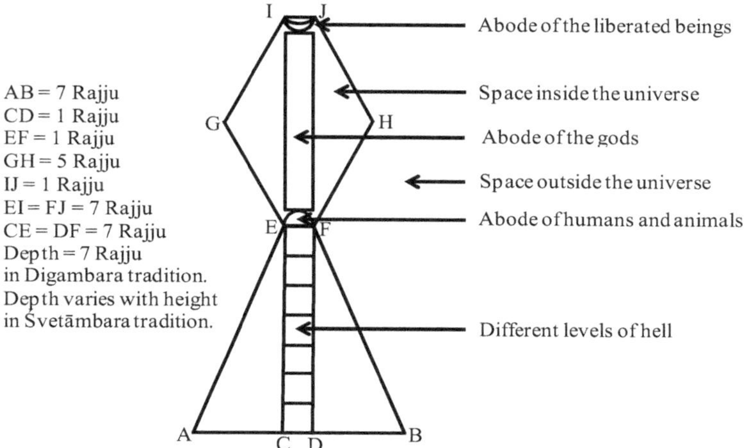

Figure 1.1: Shape of the universe in Jain tradition

1.2 Middle world

Jain texts Jambūdvīpaprajñapti, Trilokasāra, Triloka Prajñapti, Trilokadipikā, and Kṣetrasamāsa provide detailed information about the middle world and Jambudwīpa. The middle world consists of a central island, which is surrounded by alternating annular oceans and islands. The central circular island called Jambudwīpa is surrounded by an annular ocean called Lavaṇa Ocean. An annular island called Dhātakīkhaṇḍa surrounds the Lavaṇa Ocean. Dhātakīkhaṇḍa is surrounded by an annular ocean called Kālodadhi, which is again surrounded by an island called Puṣkaravara. This pattern continues till the edge of the universe. The number of these concentric islands and oceans is extremely large. The width of each successive continent or ocean is double that of previous one as shown in Table 1.2 and Figure 1.2.

Table 1.2: Islands and oceans in the middle world [Sūrya Prajñapti 19.130-157]

Islands/oceans	Width (yojana)	Number of suns	Number of moons	Number of nakṣatras
Jambudwīpa	100,000	2	2	56
Lavaṇa ocean	200,000	4	4	112
Dhātakīkhaṇḍa	400,000	12	12	336
Kālodadhi ocean	800,000	42	42	1,176
Puṣkaravara	1,600,000	144	144	4,032

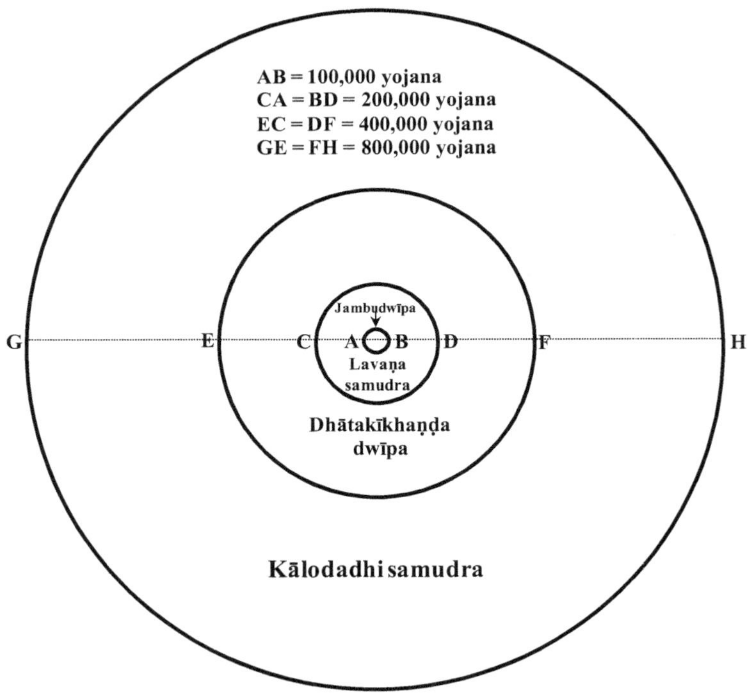

Figure 1.2: Geometry of middle world

The abode of human beings is limited to two and half islands, Jambudwīpa, Dhātakīkhaṇḍa, and inner half of Puṣkaravara.

1.3 Jambudwīpa

Located at the centre of middle world, Jambudwīpa has a diameter of 100,000 yojana. Jambudwīpa is divided in parallel regions of alternating plains and mountains as shown in Figure 1.3.

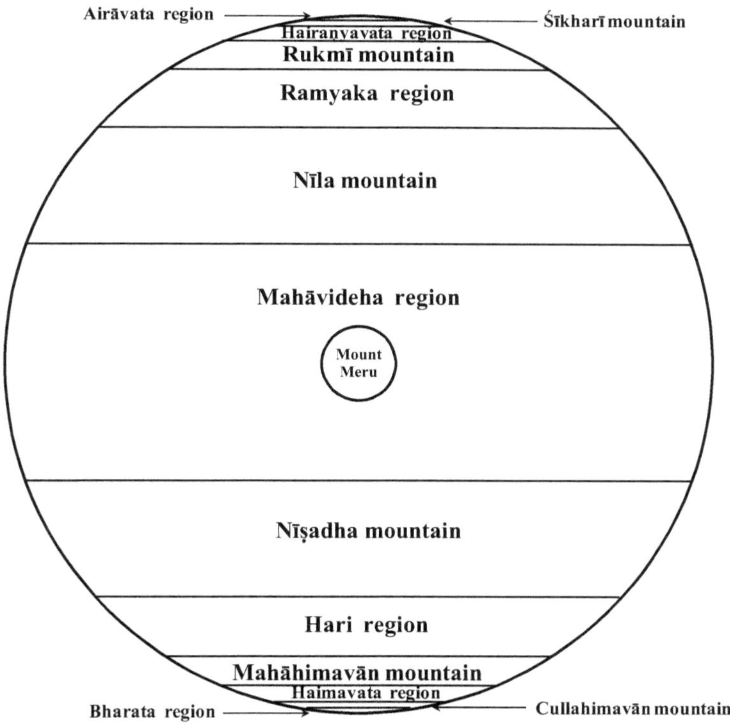

Figure 1.3: The geometry of Jambudwīpa

These regions starting from south tip of Jambudwīpa are called Bharata, Cullahimavān, Haimavata, Mahāhimavān, Hari, Niṣadha, Mahāvideha, Nīla, Ramyaka, Rukmī, Hairaṇyavata, Śikharī, and Airāvata. The widest region is the central region called Mahāvideha. The width of regions reduces by half successively on both sides of Mahāvideha region as shown in Table 1.3. In the Mahāvideha region and at the centre of Jambudwīpa is a mountain called Mount Meru as shown in Figure 1.4.

Table 1.3: The divisions of Jambudwīpa

Zone	Width (yojana)	Ratio
Bharata region	526.32	1
Cullahimavān mountain	1052.63	2
Haimavata region	2105.26	4
Mahāhimavān mountain	4210.53	8
Hari region	8421.05	16
Niṣadha mountain	16842.11	32
Mahāvideha region (central region of the Jambudwīpa)	33684.21	64
Nīla mountain	16842.11	32
Ramyaka region	8421.05	16
Rukmī mountain	4210.53	8
Hairaṇyavata region	2105.26	4
Śikharī mountain	1052.63	2
Airāvata region	526.32	1
Total	100000	190

1.4 Mount Meru

Mount Meru is 100,000 yojana in height with 99,000 yojana being above and 1000 yojana being below the top surface of Jambudwīpa as shown in Figures 1.5 and 1.6.

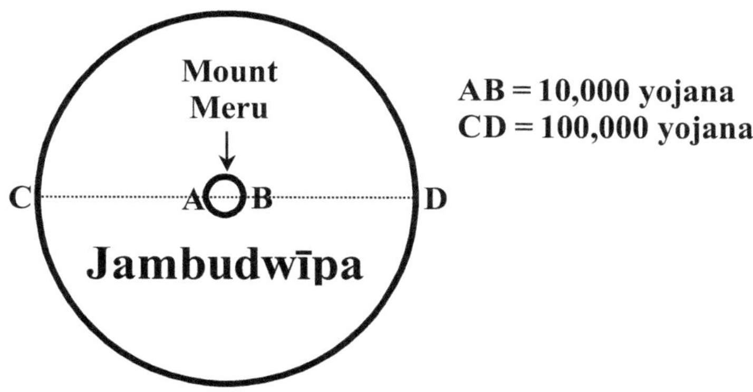

Figure 1.4: Jambudwīpa and Mount Meru

The diameter of Mount Meru at the top surface of Jambudwīpa is 10,000 yojana. The section of Mount Meru above the top surface of Jambudwīpa is divided in two parts. Thus Mount Meru has three parts, bottom part of 1000 yojana below the top surface of Jambudwīpa, middle part of 63,000 yojana above it and top part of 36,000 yojana above middle part. At the top of Mount Meru, its diameter is 1000 yojana. All the heavenly bodies including sun, moon, and stars revolve around Mount Meru.

1.5 Heavenly bodies

The suns, moons, and stars revolve around Mount Meru at fixed height from the top surface of Jambudwīpa.

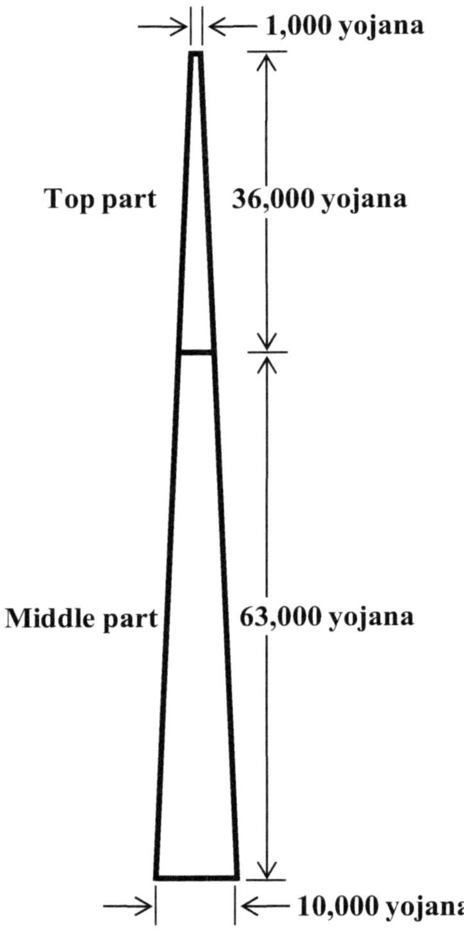

Figure 1.5: The middle and top parts of Mount Meru

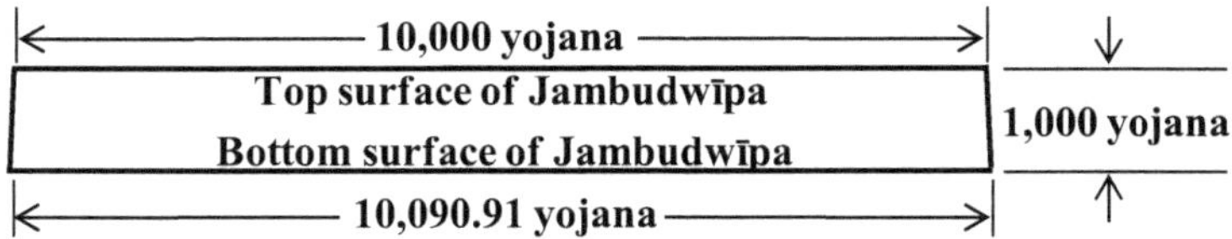

Figure 1.6: Bottom part of Mount Meru

Stars travel at two levels, lower level at 790 yojana and higher level at 900 yojana. Sun and moon travel at 800 yojana and 880 yojana respectively from the top surface of Jambudwīpa. The projection of the trajectories of sun, moon, and stars on the plane of Jambudwīpa is shown in Figure 1.7.

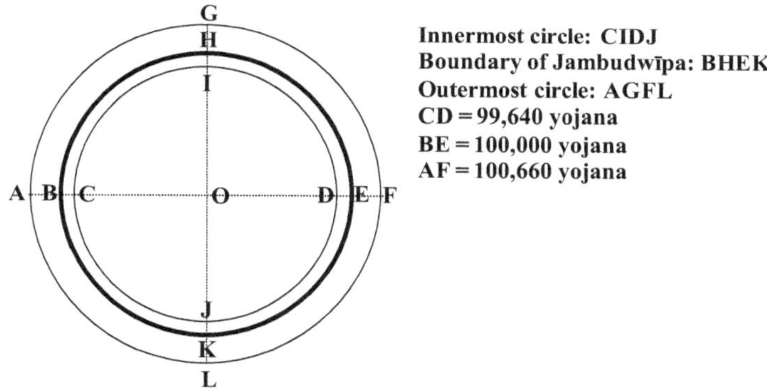

Figure 1.7: Projection of the trajectories of sun, moon, and stars on the plane of Jambudwīpa

The suns, moons, and stars belonging to Jambudwīpa travel between two circles, innermost circle at 180 yojana inside Jambudwīpa and outermost circle at 330 yojana outside Jambudwīpa. The difference in radii of innermost and outermost circles is 510 yojana. The area between the innermost and outermost circles is divided in a number of lanes for the movement of heavenly bodies. It should be noted that the numbers for distances given in Jain texts are not to be taken literally. These numbers have been carefully selected to provide a good approximation of the movement of heavenly bodies from the point of observation used by Jain astronomers at a particular epoch. In this book, the focus of research is on where and when the Jain astronomical observations were made. We will begin by identifying the centres of Jain astronomy.

Notes

1. Vijaya (1957): 10-12.
2. Conversion to modern units by the author.
3. Sridharan (2005): 7.
4. Joseph (2011): 349-354.
5. https://en.wikipedia.org/wiki/Sthananga_Sutra.
6. Stillwell (2010): 10.
7. Napier (1614).
8. Stedman (1677).
9. Gauss (1799): 361-432.
10. Pascal (1653).

"The true joy of a moonlit night is something we no longer understand. Only the men of old, when there were no lights, could understand the true joy of a moonlit night."

—Yasunari Kawabata

2. The Centres of Jain Astronomy

Jain astronomical texts provide a multitude of data that can be used to gain valuable insight into our glorious history. Jain astronomy provides a bridge between Vedic astronomy and classical Hindu astronomy. Vedāṅga Jyotiṣa is a text on Vedic astronomy that has come to us in two recensions, Ṛk Vedāṅga Jyotiṣa and Yajus Vedāṅga Jyotiṣa. According to Vedāṅga Jyotiṣa, there are 30 muhūrtas in a day and night (Ṛk Vedāṅga Jyotiṣa 16, Yajus Vedāṅga Jyotiṣa 38) and during the course of the year days and night increase or decrease by a maximum of 6 muhūrtas (Ṛk Vedāṅga Jyotiṣa 7, Yajus Vedāṅga Jyotiṣa 8). According to Jain text Jambudvīpaprajñapti 7.167, the day is 18 muhūrta long and night is 12 muhūrta, when sun is at the innermost maṇḍala (circle) of the Jambudvīpa. The day is 12 muhūrta long and night is 18 muhūrta long, when sun is at the outermost maṇḍala. From this information, it can be inferred that the innermost maṇḍala is the Tropic of Cancer and the outermost maṇḍala is the Tropic of Capricorn. Thus according to the information given in Vedāṅga Jyotiṣa and Jambudvīpaprajñapti, the ratio of daylight duration to night duration was 1.5 on summer solstice, longest day of the year, and the ratio of night duration to daylight duration was 1.5 on winter solstice, the shortest day of the year. The ratio of longest daylight duration to shortest night duration is a function of latitude, and this information can be used to locate the place where this observation was made [1].

2.1 The seat of learning

Some scholars have proposed that this information was borrowed by Indians from Babylonians or Greeks as described below:

> Characteristic of the middle period is the fact that the longest day is considered independent of the geographic latitude and that the ratio of the longest day to the shortest day is taken to be 3:2. This ratio corresponds to a geographic latitude of almost 34°, too high for all parts of India except the northwestern corner. THIBAUT mentions that this ratio might be of Babylonian origin but considers this very unlikely because textual evidence was not available. In the meantime, however, KUGLER discovered that the ratio 3:2 occurs in Babylonian cuneiform texts of the Seleucid period. This, coupled with the fact that the ratio of 3:2 was considered in antiquity characteristic for the climate of Babylon, makes it very plausible that the ratio was taken over by the Hindus without correction. [2]
>
> The ratio 3:2 used by the Indians, however, was commonly utilized in all Babylonian astronomical texts after ca 700 B.C. This tradition must surely be the source of the Sanskrit texts under discussion, and provide us with a terminus post quem for those texts. [3]

Based on the nakṣatra positions given in the Vedāṅga Jyotiṣa, the Vedāṅga Jyotiṣa is currently dated to 1150 BCE to 1400 BCE [4]. Since Vedāṅga Jyotiṣa is over 450 years older than Babylonian texts even by the most conservative estimate, it is more likely that the ratio of 1.5 was borrowed by Babylonians from Indians. The idea that this ratio was borrowed by Indians is based on the wrong notion that there is no prominent place in India where this ratio is valid. Even in the quote above by Schmidt [2], it is said that this ratio is valid for north western part of the then united India. This fact is conveniently ignored to proclaim that the ratio of 3:2 was borrowed from Babylonian astronomers. Kuppanna Sastry in his translation of Vedāṅga Jyotiṣa has also noted that the ratio of 1.5 refers to 35 degrees latitude in the extreme north of India [4]. Sharma and Lishk have also argued against the foreign influence on Indian astronomy and proposed that the ratio 3:2 fits the region of Gandhāra as well and was discovered independently.

> Besides, the simplicity of the relation between the ratio 3:2 and 183 days (half the annual course of the Sun) suggests that the Jainas might have searched for a standard place like Gandhāra where a simple relation of this order holds good. … Gandhāra had been a renowned seat of ancient Indian culture, and no abode of any mythological creatures. As Gandhāra and Babylon are situated on latitudes very close to each other, the ratio 3:2 might have been found independently in these two places. [5]

Gandhāra was a kingdom in ancient India. Its most important cities were Puruṣapura (current Peshawar), Puṣkalāvatī (current Charsadda) and Takṣaśilā (current Taxila). The identification of Gandhāra fits the ratio 3:2 well, however, Gandhāra was a wide region. Sharma and

Lishk specify a ratio of 1.42 for Gandhāra, but do not specify exactly where in Gandhāra this ratio holds good. It can be shown using modern astronomical calculations that the ratio of 3:2 fits the location of Taxila exactly, which has latitude of 33.74° and longitude of 72.80°.

The duration of daylight and night for any day of the year at any location in the world can be obtained from U.S. Naval Observatory website [6]. Table 2.1 shows the duration of daylight and night on the 21st day of each month at Taxila. This data is converted into the ratios of the duration of daylight to night and vice-versa in Table 2.2. The data is shown graphically in Figures 2.1 and 2.2.

Table 2.1: Duration of daylight and night at Taxila

		Daylight		Night	
Month	Date	Hour	Minute	Hour	Minute
1	21 January, 2017	10	17	13	43
2	21 February, 2017	11	12	12	48
3	21 March, 2017	12	10	11	50
4	21 April, 2017	13	13	10	47
5	21 May, 2017	14	3	9	57
6	**21 June, 2017**	**14**	**24**	**9**	**36**
7	21 July, 2017	14	4	9	56
8	21 August, 2017	13	13	10	47
9	21 September, 2017	12	11	11	49
10	21 October, 2017	11	10	12	50
11	21 November, 2017	10	17	13	43
12	**21 December, 2017**	**9**	**55**	**14**	**5**

Table 2.2: The ratio of daylight duration to night duration (D/N) and vice versa (N/D) at Taxila

Month	Date	D/N	N/D
1	21 January, 2017	0.75	1.33
2	21 February, 2017	0.88	1.14
3	21 March, 2017	1.03	0.97
4	21 April, 2017	1.23	0.82
5	21 May, 2017	1.41	0.71
6	**21 June, 2017**	**1.50**	0.67
7	21 July, 2017	1.42	0.71
8	21 August, 2017	1.23	0.82
9	21 September, 2017	1.03	0.97
10	21 October, 2017	0.87	1.15
11	21 November, 2017	0.75	1.33
12	**21 December, 2017**	0.70	**1.42**

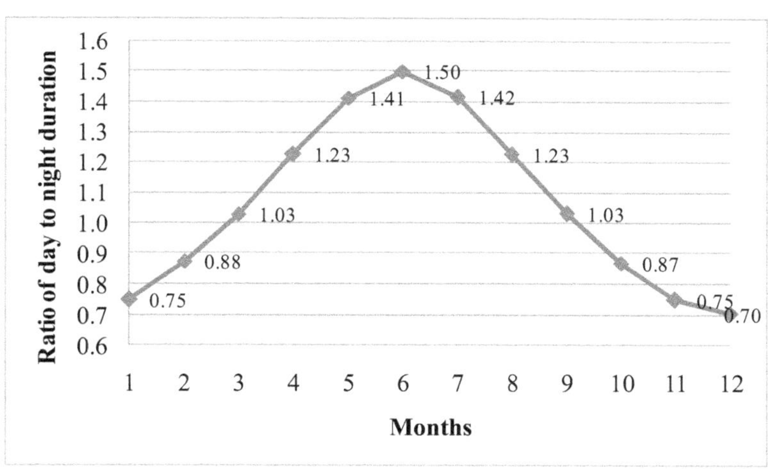

Figure 2.1: The ratio of daylight duration to night duration at Taxila

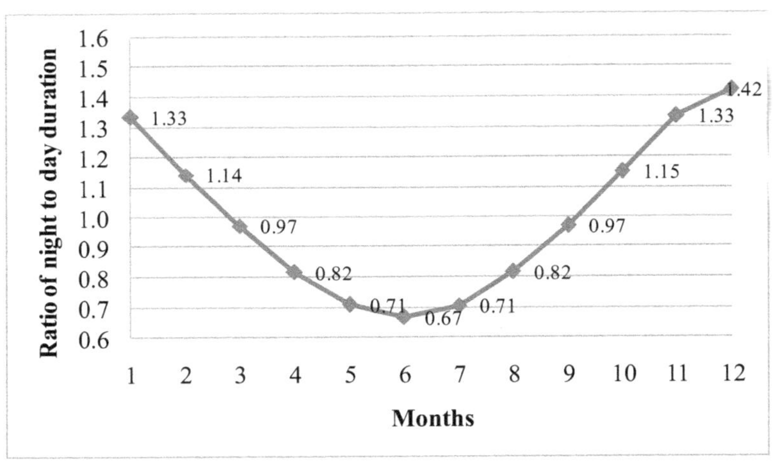

Figure 2.2: The ratio of night duration to daylight duration at Taxila

The choice of 21st day of each month is based on the fact that summer and winter solstices as well as vernal and autumnal equinoxes take place around 21st of the respective months. Months 1 to 12 in these Tables and Figures refer to months January to December respectively.

From Table 2.2 and Figure 2.1, it can be seen that the ratio of daylight duration to night duration at Taxila on summer solstice is 1.5 and matches exactly with the ratio given in Vedāṅga Jyotiṣa and Jambudvīpaprajñapti. From Table 2.2 and Figure 2.2, it can be seen that the ratio of night duration to daylight duration on winter solstice at Taxila is 1.42 and close to the value of 1.5 given in Vedāṅga Jyotiṣa and Jambudvīpaprajñapti. Since the data has been obtained for the year 2017, it is natural to ask whether this data is applicable to the observations made during 2nd millennium

BCE. The duration of daylight is a function of latitude and tilt of earth's axis to the ecliptic. For fixed latitude, the duration over long time will only depend on earth's tilt. Earth's tilt is currently approximately 23.5 degrees. According to NASA Earth Observatory website [7], earth's tilt changes from 22.1 to 24.5 degrees over a period of 40,000 years. Over a 40,000 year cycle, earth's tilt changes by only 2.4 degrees. As the Vedāṅga Jyotiṣa was written in second millennium BCE (less than 4,000 years from present), the earth's tilt could have differed by no more than 0.24 degrees from the present during the time of the Vedāṅga Jyotiṣa and the duration of daylight would not have been significantly different from the values we have now.

From the discussion above, it is clear that there is a specific location in ancient India, namely Taxila, where the observations about the ratios of day and night durations are satisfied. Taxila was the most ancient centre of learning in India with the famous Takṣaśilā University located there. This identification shows that Taxila was the original centre of Vedic astronomy and Jain astronomy. It is important to note that Taxila is located in the area where Indus Valley Civilization flourished. This discovery points to the continuity of ancient Indian Civilization. As the time passed by, another centre of Jain astronomy emerged, which occupied a prominent place in Indian history. This seat of learning was Ujjain, and its prominence was related to its specific location in India. Ancient India was a knowledge-based civilization and ancient Indians went to great lengths to preserve their knowledge and pass it on to future generations. Both Jains and Hindus created several myths to propagate their knowledge, and one of the most endearing of those myths is the legend of Vikramāditya.

2.2 The Legends of Vikramāditya

Indian tradition recognizes Emperor Vikramāditya as the greatest ruler of India. The Vikrama era of 57 BCE constituted in his memory continues to be used in India symbolizing the love and affection people have for him even though more than 2000 years have passed since he left this mortal world. Modern history has denied the very existence of this great emperor and some minor king named Azes has been credited for instituting the Vikrama era. There are a number of legends about Vikramāditya that have made him the darling of the masses. Some of these legends are based on historical persons, and some of them have scientific meanings behind them.

The memory of Vikramāditya has been preserved in the literary traditions of Hindus such as the Gāthāsaptaśatī composed by Hāla Sātavāhana, Bṛhatkathā composed by Guṇāḍhya, Bṛhatkathāmañjarī composed by Kṣemendra, and Kathāsaritsāgara composed by Somadeva. The last two texts are based on Bṛhatkathā, which was originally written in Paiśāchī Prākṛta and is not available now. The adventures of Vikramāditya have been popularized in a number of books of fiction such as Vetālapañchaviṃśati (popularly known as Vetāla Pachīsī), Siṃhāsana-dwātṛṃśikā (popularly known as Siṃhāsana Battīsī) and Śuka-saptaśatī (popularly known as the story of the "Parrot and Mynah").

The story of Vikramāditya and his family is also described in many Jain texts such as Paṭṭāvalīs, Harivaṃśa, and

Prabhāvakacharita composed by Prabhāchandra, Prabandhakoṣa composed by Rājaśekhara, Prabandha Chintāmaṇi composed by Merutuṅga Sūri, Purātana Prabandha Saṃgraha and Vikrama Charitra composed by Devamūrti, Vikrama Charitra composed by Śubhaśīla, and Vikrama Pañchadaṇḍa Prabandha composed by Rāmachandra Sūri.

Vikramāditya was the legendary king of Ujjain, known in ancient times as Ujjayinī, which was the capital of the Malwa region. It was known as Anādi Ujjayinī, a city without beginning in time. Ujjayinī received several names over time, one of which was Avantikā for being the capital of the kingdom of Avanti. Avantikā is among the seven holy cities, which are considered the doorway to salvation, according to Hindu scriptures. Another name for Ujjain was Viśālā, a name by which Kālidāsa refers to this city in Meghadūta. He says, "O Cloud, when you go to Avanti, go to the city of Viśālā, where elders tell the story of Udayana. This city looks like a gleaming part of heaven that people from heaven have brought with them with their remaining meritorious deeds." The story of Udayana, the daring king of Vatsa, and Vāsavadattā, the ethereally beautiful princess of Avanti, is the most endearing love story of ancient India, which formed the basis of many literary works. A long time ago, Ujjayinī was considered to be at the centre of the universe. We can't be sure of that, but Ujjayinī certainly is located at a very special place in India. It was realized very early in the history of India that Ujjayinī was located at the Tropic of Cancer. It was this location at the Tropic of Cancer that formed the basis of the legend of Vikramāditya.

Traditionally, it is assumed that the word Vikramāditya is composed by joining the words "Vikrama" and "Āditya". Vikrama means valour, and Āditya means Sun, and thus the meaning of Vikramāditya is the "Sun of Valour" or "Brave as the Sun". However, this was not the intended meaning behind the legend of Vikramāditya. The word Vikramāditya can also be composed by joining the prefix "Vi" with the words "Krama" and "Āditya". The prefix "Vi" imparts the meaning of deviation or opposite to the word that follows it. For example, the word "Vikāra" means creating deviation and hence connotes degradation. The word "Kraya" means to buy and the word "Vikraya" means to sell. The word "Krama" means "order" and "Āditya" of course means the Sun. Putting it all together, Vikramāditya means deviation in the order of the Sun. Let us ponder at what happens to the Sun at Ujjayinī. During the summer months, the Sun moves northwards towards Ujjayinī and continues till the day of the summer solstice, on which day the Sun stands vertically up at Ujjayinī. The next day the Sun reverses its journey and starts going south. This fact that the Sun changes its course at Ujjayinī, formed the basis of the legend of Vikramāditya. It was because of its location at the Tropic of Cancer that Ujjayinī became the most prominent centre for astronomical research in ancient India. It also became the place from which time was synchronized all over India. It became the prime meridian of the ancient world in the manner of Greenwich today. Bhāskara-I has written that the prime meridian passes through Laṅkā, Vātsyapura, Avanti, Sthāneśvara, and abode of the gods [8]. Other ancient Indian astronomers have specified many other points on this meridian, and so there is no doubt about the intended meaning. Here, the abode of the gods is Mount Meru, which is the astronomical term for the North Pole. Laṅkā here does not represent any city in Sri Lanka, but a point at the intersection of the equator and the meridian passing through Ujjain. This point is in the Indian Ocean, far away from Sri Lanka. As time all over India was synchronized from the time in Ujjayinī, the Lord of Ujjayinī was made Mahākāla or "Time, the Great" from Mahā meaning "great" and Kāla meaning "time". Ujjayinī is famous for the temple of Mahākāla, who is identified with Lord Śiva now.

Ujjayinī was to ancient India, what Greenwich is to modern world. It was Ujjain (Ujjayinī) where the centre of Jain astronomy shifted from the original centre in Taxila (Takṣaśilā). To properly understand the information given in Jain astronomical texts, the identification of the centres of Jain astronomy is vital, because the sky looks different based on the location of the observer.

Notes:

1. Roy (2018c).
2. Schmidt (1944).
3. Pingree (1973).
4. Kuppanna Sastry (1985): 13-14.
5. Sharma and Lishk (1979).
6. http://aa.usno.navy.mil/data/docs/Dur_OneYear.php.
7. https://earthobservatory.nasa.gov/Features/Milankovitch/milankovitch_2.php.
8. Laghubhāskarīya 1.23.

"Order and simplification are the first steps toward the mastery of a subject."
- Thomas Mann

3. The Division of Sky

The most fundamental concept of Indian astronomy is that of nakṣatra. It takes the moon ~27.32 days to return to the same position among the stars. Based on this measurement, the path of moon in the background of the stars was divided in 28 or 27 divisions, each division being called a nakṣatra or lunar mansion. Atharvaveda Saṃhitā (19.7.1-5) lists the 28 nakṣatras as follows:

> 1. Seeking favour of the twenty-eight fold wondrous ones, shining in the sky together, ever-moving, hasting in the creation (Bhūvana), I worship (sapary) with songs the days, the firmament (nāka).
> 2. Easy of invocation for me [be] the Kṛttikās and Rohiṇī; be Mṛgaśirās excellent, [and] Ārdrā healthful (Śām); be the two Punarvasus pleasantness, Pushya what is agreeable, the Āśleṣās light (Bhānu), the Maghās progress (āyana) [for me].
> 3. Be the former Phālgunīs and Hasta here auspicious (puṇyam); be Chitrā propitious, and Svāti easy (sukhā) for me; be the two Viśākhās bestowal (rādhas), Anurādhā easy of invocation, Jyeshṭhā a good asterism, Mūla uninjured.
> 4. Let the former Ashāḍhās give me food; let the latter ones bring refreshment; let Abhijit give me what is

> auspicious; let Śrāvaṇa [and] the Śravishṭhās make good prosperity.
> 5. Let Śatabhishaj [bring] to me what is great widely; let the double Proshṭhapadas [bring] to me good protection (suśarman]; let Revatī and the two Aśvayuj [bring] fortune to me; let the Bharaṇīs bring to me wealth. [1]

Based on the above text, the list of 28 nakṣatras is shown in Table 3.1. The nakṣatra Abhijit was later dropped in Vedic/Hindu astronomy and the system of 27 nakṣatras became standard. However, Jains kept Abhijit nakṣatra and Jain astronomy is based on the concept of 28 nakṣatras. There is a dialogue between Indra and Skanda regarding the dropping of Abhijit nakṣatra in Mahābhārata (Vana Parva, 230: 8-10). In this dialogue, Indra says to Skanda that because of jealousy with Rohiṇī, her younger sister Abhijit has gone to forest to do penance. This is a figurative way of saying that Abhijit has been dropped from the list of nakṣatras. There was also a change in the yogatārā of Revatī nakṣatra. This is figuratively told in the story of dropping of Revatī and her reinstatement as described in Chapter 72 of Mārkaṇḍeya Puarāṇa.

Each nakṣatra was assigned a presiding deity or set of deities in Vedic astronomy. The list of 27 nakṣatras with their deity/deities is given in the Taittirīya Saṃhitā (iv.4.10) as follows:

> (Thou art) Krittikas, the Naksatra, Agni, the deity; … (Thou art) Rohini the Naksatra, Prajapati the deity; Mrigaśirsa the Naksatra, Soma the deity; Ardra the Naksatra, Rudra the deity; the two Punarvasus the Naksatra, Aditi the deity; Tisya the Naksatra, Brihaspati the deity; the Aśresas the Naksatra, the serpents the

> deity; the Maghas the Naksatra, the fathers the deity; the two Phalgunis the Naksatra, Aryaman the deity; the two Phalgunis the Naksatra, Bhaga the deity; Hasta the Naksatra, Savitr the deity; Chitra the Naksatra, Indra the deity; Svati the Naksatra, Vayu the deity; the two Viśakhas the Naksatra, Indra and Agni the deity; Anruradha the Naksatra, Mitra the deity; Rohini the Naksatra, Indra the deity; the two Viśrits the Naksatra; the fathers the deity; the Asadhas the Naksatra, the waters the deity; the Asadhas the Naksatra, the All-gods the deity; Śrona the Naksatra, Visnu the deity; Śravistha the Naksatra, the Vasus the, deity; Śatabhisaj the Naksatra, Indra the deity; Prosthapadas the Naksatra, the goat of one foot the deity; the Prosthapadas the Naksatra, the serpent of the deep the deity; Revati the Naksatra, Pusan the deity; the two Aśvayujs the Naksatra, the Aśvins the deity; the Apabharanis the Naksatra, Yama the deity. [2]

Based on the above text, the presiding deities of the nakṣatras are shown in Table 3.1. The list of the presiding deities of 27 nakṣatras is also given in Vedāṅga Jyotiṣa, the earliest known astronomical text of India [3]. Table 3.1 lists the presiding deities as given in Vedāṅga Jyotiṣa as well [4]. The names of nakṣatras are same in Jain astronomy, but the list starts with Abhijit nakṣatra according to Jambudwīpa Prajñapti [5]. Jambudwīpa Prajñapti also lists the deities and gotras (ancestor sages) of each nakṣatra. Table 3.2 lists the nakṣatras, their presiding deities, and their gotras as given in Jambudwīpa Prajñapti [6].

Table 3.1: List of nakṣatras in Vedic astronomy [4]

	Nakṣatras		Nakṣatras	Deities (Taittirīya Saṃhitā)	Deities (Vedāṅga Jyotiṣa)
1.	Kṛttikā	1.	Kṛttikā	Agni	Agni
2.	Rohiṇī	2.	Rohiṇī	Prajāpati	Prajāpati
3.	Mṛgaśirā	3.	Mṛgaśīrṣa	Soma	Soma
4.	Ārdrā	4.	Ārdrā	Rudra	Rudra
5.	Punarvasu	5.	Punarvasu	Aditi	Aditi
6.	Puṣya	6.	Tiṣhya	Bṛhaspati	Bṛhaspati
7.	Āśleṣā	7.	Āśreshā	Serpents	Serpents
8.	Maghā	8.	Maghā	Fathers	Fathers
9.	Pūrva-Phālgunī	9.	(Pūrva) Phālgunī	Aryamā	Bhaga
10.	Uttara-Phālgunī	10.	(Uttara) Phālgunī	Bhaga	Aryaman
11.	Hasta	11.	Hasta	Savitā	Savitā
12.	Citrā	12.	Citrā	Indra	Tvasṭā
13.	Svāti	13.	Svātī	Vayu	Vayu
14.	Viśākhā	14.	Viśākhā	Indra and Agni	Indra and Agni
15.	Anurādhā	15.	Anurādhā	Mitra	Mitra
16.	Jyeṣṭhā	16.	Rohiṇī	Indra	Indra
17.	Mūla	17.	Vichṛta	Fathers	Nirṛti
18.	Pūrvāṣāḍhā	18.	(Pūrva) Āshāḍhā	Waters	Waters
19.	Uttarāṣāḍhā	19.	(Uttara) Āshāḍhā	All-gods	All-gods
20.	Abhijit				
21.	Śravaṇa	20.	Śroṇa	Viṣṇu	Viṣṇu
22.	Śraviṣṭhā	21.	Śraviṣṭhā	Vasu	Vasu
23.	Śatabhiṣaja	22.	Śatabhiṣaja	Indra	Varuṇa
24.	Pūrva-Proshṭhapadā	23.	(Pūrva) Proshṭhapadā	Goat of one foot	Goat of one foot
25.	Uttara-Proshṭhapadā	24.	(Uttara) Proshṭhapadā	Serpent of the deep	Serpent of the deep
26.	Revatī	25.	Revatī	Pushā	Pushan
27.	Aśvayuja	26.	Aśvayuja	Aśvins	Aśvins
28.	Bharaṇī	27.	Apabharaṇī	Yama	Yama

Table 3.2: Nakṣatras and their deities in Jain astronomy [6]

	Nakṣatras	Deities	Gotra (lineage)
1.	Abhijit	Brahmā	Modgalāyana
2.	Śravaṇa	Viṣṇu	Sāṅkhyāyana
3.	Dhaniṣṭhā	Vasu	Agrabhāva
4.	Śatabhiṣaja	Varuṇa	Karṇilāyana
5.	Pūrvabhādrapadā	Goat of one foot	Jātukarṇa
6.	Uttarabhādrapadā	Abhivṛddhi	Dhananjaya
7.	Revatī	Puṣā	Puṣyāyana
8.	Aświnī	Aśva	Aśvāyana
9.	Bharaṇī	Yama	Bhārgaveśa
10.	Kṛttikā	Agni	Agniveśma
11.	Rohiṇī	Prajāpati	Gautama
12.	Mṛgaśirā	Soma	Bhārdwāja
13.	Ārdrā	Rudra	Lohityāyana
14.	Punarvasu	Aditi	Vasiṣṭha
15.	Puṣya	Bṛhaspati	Avamārjāyana
16.	Āśleṣā	Serpents	Māṇḍavyāyana
17.	Maghā	Fathers	Piṅgāyana
18.	Pūrvaphālgunī	Bhaga	Govalya
19.	Uttaraphālgunī	Aryamā	Kaśyapa
20.	Hasta	Savitā	Kauśika
21.	Citrā	Tvaṣṭā	Dārbhāyana
22.	Svātī	Vayu	Cāmaracchāyana
23.	Viśākhā	Indra and Agni	Śuṅgāyana
24.	Anurādhā	Mitra	Govalyāyana
25.	Jyeṣṭhā	Indra	Cikitsāyana
26.	Mūla	Nerṛta	Kātyāyana
27.	Pūrvāṣāḍhā	Waters	Bābhravyāyana
28.	Uttarāṣāḍhā	All-gods	Vyāghrāpatya

One of the distinguishing features of Jain astronomy is the unequal division of 28 nakṣatras compared to equal division of 27 nakṣatras in Hindu astronomy. Since earlier Vedic texts refer to 28 nakṣatras, it stands to reason that Jain astronomers have preserved the original division of nakṣatras, which were unequal in span. This may explain why many conjunction stars (yogatārās) of nakṣatras fall outside of their nakṣatras in Hindu astronomy.

Jain astronomical texts such as Triloka Prajñapti and Jambudwīpa Prajñapti provide detailed information to calculate the span of each nakṣatra. These texts provide the information in three different ways, which yield identical results. Jain texts divide the sky in 54,900 parts called gaganakhaṇḍa or portions of sky. Table 3.3 shows the respective portions of sky in each nakṣatra according to Jain astronomy and the fractional span of each nakṣatra based on this information. Jain texts also provide the time it takes for the moon during its monthly journey and the sun during its yearly journey to traverse across each nakṣatra. This information is shown in Tables 3.4 and 3.5. The calculated values of the fractional times spent by the moon and the sun in each nakṣatra are also shown in Tables 3.4 and 3.5. It can be seen that Jain astronomers made careful calculations to provide consistent information based on three different methods. The fractional span of each nakṣatra can be converted to the span of each nakṣatra in sky as shown in Table 3.6. Based on the span of each nakṣatra, the ecliptic longitudes of the beginning and end of each nakṣatra can be calculated and are shown in Table 3.6 as well.

Table 3.3: Nakṣatras and their spans in sky according to Jain astronomy [7]

	Nakṣatras	Parts in sky	Fractional span
1.	Abhijit	630	0.0115
2.	Śravaṇa	2010	0.0366
3.	Dhaniṣṭhā	2010	0.0366
4.	Śatabhiṣaja	1005	0.0183
5.	Pūrvabhādrapadā	2010	0.0366
6.	Uttarabhādrapadā	3015	0.0549
7.	Revatī	2010	0.0366
8.	Aświnī	2010	0.0366
9.	Bharaṇī	1005	0.0183
10.	Kṛttikā	2010	0.0366
11.	Rohiṇī	3015	0.0549
12.	Mṛgaśirā	2010	0.0366
13.	Ārdrā	1005	0.0183
14.	Punarvasu	3015	0.0549
15.	Puṣya	2010	0.0366
16.	Āśleṣā	1005	0.0183
17.	Maghā	2010	0.0366
18.	Pūrvaphālgunī	2010	0.0366
19.	Uttaraphālgunī	3015	0.0549
20.	Hasta	2010	0.0366
21.	Citrā	2010	0.0366
22.	Svātī	1005	0.0183
23.	Viśākhā	3015	0.0549
24.	Anurādhā	2010	0.0366
25.	Jyeṣṭhā	1005	0.0183
26.	Mūla	2010	0.0366
27.	Pūrvāṣāḍhā	2010	0.0366
28.	Uttarāṣāḍhā	3015	0.0549
	Total	54900	

Table 3.4: Time spent (muhūrta) by moon in each nakṣatra during one lunar month according to Jain astronomy [8]

	Nakṣatras	Time spent (muhūrta) in each nakṣatra	Fractional time (time in nakṣatra/total time)
1.	Abhijit	9 and 27/67	0.0115
2.	Śravaṇa	30	0.0366
3.	Dhaniṣṭhā	30	0.0366
4.	Śatabhiṣaja	15	0.0183
5.	Pūrvabhādrapadā	30	0.0366
6.	Uttarabhādrapadā	45	0.0549
7.	Revatī	30	0.0366
8.	Aświnī	30	0.0366
9.	Bharaṇī	15	0.0183
10.	Kṛttikā	30	0.0366
11.	Rohiṇī	45	0.0549
12.	Mṛgaśirā	30	0.0366
13.	Ārdrā	15	0.0183
14.	Punarvasu	45	0.0549
15.	Puṣya	30	0.0366
16.	Āśleṣā	15	0.0183
17.	Maghā	30	0.0366
18.	Pūrvaphālgunī	30	0.0366
19.	Uttaraphālgunī	45	0.0549
20.	Hasta	30	0.0366
21.	Citrā	30	0.0366
22.	Svātī	15	0.0183
23.	Viśākhā	45	0.0549
24.	Anurādhā	30	0.0366
25.	Jyeṣṭhā	15	0.0183
26.	Mūla	30	0.0366
27.	Pūrvāṣāḍhā	30	0.0366
28.	Uttarāṣāḍhā	45	0.0549
	Total	819 and 27/67	

Table 3.5: Time spent by sun in each nakṣatra during one year according to Jain astronomy [9]

	Nakṣatras	Time spent (Muhūrta) in each nakṣatra	Fractional time (time in nakṣatra/total time)
1.	Abhijit	126	0.0115
2.	Śravaṇa	402	0.0366
3.	Dhaniṣṭhā	402	0.0366
4.	Śatabhiṣaja	201	0.0183
5.	Pūrvabhādrapadā	402	0.0366
6.	Uttarabhādrapadā	603	0.0549
7.	Revatī	402	0.0366
8.	Aświnī	402	0.0366
9.	Bharaṇī	201	0.0183
10.	Kṛttikā	402	0.0366
11.	Rohiṇī	603	0.0549
12.	Mṛgaśirā	402	0.0366
13.	Ārdrā	201	0.0183
14.	Punarvasu	603	0.0549
15.	Puṣya	402	0.0366
16.	Āśleṣā	201	0.0183
17.	Maghā	402	0.0366
18.	Pūrvaphālgunī	402	0.0366
19.	Uttaraphālgunī	603	0.0549
20.	Hasta	402	0.0366
21.	Citrā	402	0.0366
22.	Svātī	201	0.0183
23.	Viśākhā	603	0.0549
24.	Anurādhā	402	0.0366
25.	Jyeṣṭhā	201	0.0183
26.	Mūla	402	0.0366
27.	Pūrvāṣāḍhā	402	0.0366
28.	Uttarāṣāḍhā	603	0.0549
	Total	10980	

Table 3.6: Angular span and coordinates of nakṣatras according to Jain astronomy

	Nakṣatras	Span	Ecliptic longitudes	
			Beginning	End
1.	Abhijit	4° 7′52.1″	0° 0′0″	4° 7′52.1″
2.	Śravaṇa	13° 10′ 49.2″	4° 7′52.1″	17° 18′41.3″
3.	Dhaniṣṭhā	13° 10′ 49.2″	17° 18′41.3″	30° 29′30.5″
4.	Śatabhiṣaja	6° 35′24.6″	30° 29′30.5″	37° 4′55.1″
5.	Pūrvabhādrapadā	13° 10′ 49.2″	37° 4′55.1″	50° 15′44.3″
6.	Uttarabhādrapadā	19° 46′13.8″	50° 15′44.3″	70° 1′58.0″
7.	Revatī	13° 10′ 49.2″	70° 1′58.0″	83° 12′47.2″
8.	Aświnī	13° 10′ 49.2″	83° 12′47.2″	96° 23′36.4″
9.	Bharaṇī	6° 35′24.6″	96° 23′36.4″	102° 59′1.0″
10.	Kṛttikā	13° 10′ 49.2″	102° 59′1.0″	116° 9′50.2″
11.	Rohiṇī	19° 46′13.8″	116° 9′50.2″	135° 56′3.9″
12.	Mṛgaśirā	13° 10′ 49.2″	135° 56′3.9″	149° 6′53.1″
13.	Ārdrā	6° 35′24.6″	149° 6′53.1″	155° 42′17.7″
14.	Punarvasu	19° 46′13.8″	155° 42′17.7″	175° 28′ 31.5″
15.	Puṣya	13° 10′ 49.2″	175° 28′ 31.5″	188° 39′ 20.7″
16.	Āśleṣā	6° 35′24.6″	188° 39′ 20.7″	195° 14′ 45.2″
17.	Maghā	13° 10′ 49.2″	195° 14′ 45.2″	208° 25′ 34.4″
18.	Pūrvaphālgunī	13° 10′ 49.2″	208° 25′ 34.4″	221° 36′23.6″
19.	Uttaraphālgunī	19° 46′13.8″	221° 36′23.6″	241° 22′37.4″
20.	Hasta	13° 10′ 49.2″	241° 22′37.4″	254° 33′26.6″
21.	Citrā	13° 10′ 49.2″	254° 33′26.6″	267° 44′15.7″
22.	Swātī	6° 35′24.6″	267° 44′15.7″	274° 19′40.3″
23.	Viśākhā	19° 46′13.8″	274° 19′40.3″	294° 5′54.1″
24.	Anurādhā	13° 10′ 49.2″	294° 5′54.1″	307° 16′43.3″
25.	Jyeṣṭhā	6° 35′24.6″	307° 16′43.3″	313° 52′7.9″
26.	Mūla	13° 10′ 49.2″	313° 52′7.9″	327° 2′57.0″
27.	Pūrvāṣāḍhā	13° 10′ 49.2″	327° 2′57.0″	340° 13′46.2″
28.	Uttarāṣāḍhā	19° 46′13.8″	340° 13′46.2″	360° 0′0″

Figures 3.1 and 3.2 illustrate the equal division of 27 nakṣatras in Hindu astronomy and the unequal division of 28 nakṣatras in Jain astronomy respectively. Jain astronomical text Jambudwīpa Prajñapti also provides information on the number of stars in each nakṣatra and the shape of each nakṣatra. In addition, it provides information on the relative positions of stars in the nakṣatra with respect to the position of moon as the moon goes around the sky.

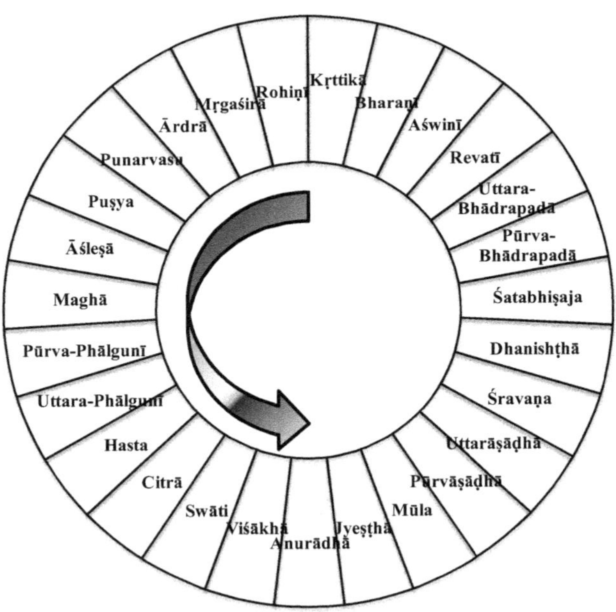

Figure 3.1: The order and equal span of 27 nakṣatras in Vedic astronomy

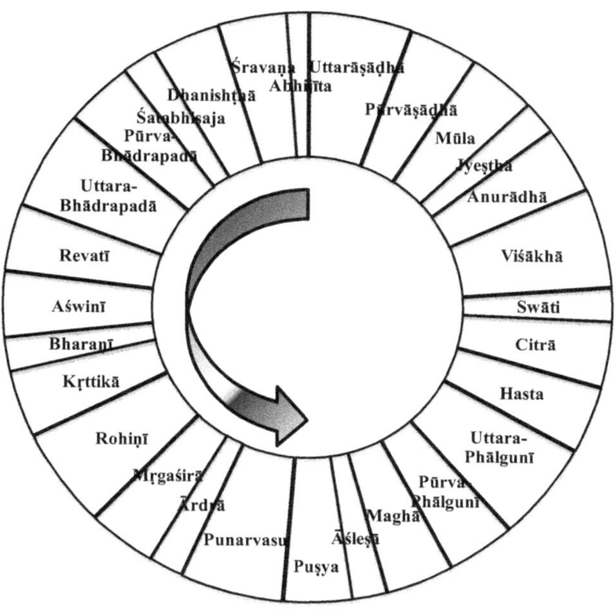

Figure 3.2: The order and unequal span of 28 nakṣatras in Jain astronomy

This additional information in combination with the span of each nakṣatra, and the coordinates of the beginning and end of each nakṣatra derived in this chapter can be used to identify the stars belonging to each nakṣatra. The correct identification of the stars belonging to each nakṣatra is not only important by itself, but also due to its significance in determining the date of the composition of Jain texts. In the next chapter we will discuss the identification of nakṣatra stars based on the astronomical information provided in Hindu and Jain texts.

Notes:

1. Whitney (1905): 907-909.
2. Keith (1914): 349.
3. Ṛk Vedāṅga Jyotisha 25-28 and Yajus Vedāṅga Jyotiṣa 32-35.
4. Atharvaveda Saṃhitā 19.7.1-5; Taittirīya Saṃhitā iv.4.10; and Ṛk Vedāṅga Jyotisha 25-28 and Yajus Vedāṅga Jyotiṣa 32-35
5. Jambudwīpa Prajñapti 7.188.
6. Jambudwīpa Prajñapti 7.188, 7.190, and 7.192.
7. Triloka Prajñapti 7.472-474.
8. Jambudwīpa Prajñapti 7.193.
9. Jambudwīpa Prajñapti 7.193.

"Look up at the stars and not down at your feet. Try to make sense of what you see, and wonder about what makes the universe exist."

— Stephen Hawking

4. Identification of Nakṣatra Stars

Based on his assumption that coordinates given in Sūrya Siddhānta are polar longitudes and latitudes, Burgess [1] identified the yogatārās as shown in Table 4.1. These identifications are currently accepted by most scholars. Ecliptic coordinates (J2000.0) of these yogatārās are also given in Table 4.1. The data for ecliptic coordinates (J2000.0) were obtained using Stellarium software by setting the date to January 1, 2000 at 12:00 noon and noting the ecliptic longitudes and latitudes by selecting the specific stars. Some astronomical texts give the number of stars in each nakṣatra. Table 4.2 shows the number of stars in each nakṣatra according to Nakṣatrakalpa of Atharvaveda, Śārdūlakarṇāvadāna, and Gargasaṃhitā as compiled by Pingree and Morrissey [2] and Jain text Jambudwīpa Prajñapti 7.191. The stars belonging to these nakṣatra star groups have been listed by Kaye [3]. Out of these star groups, yogatārās have also been specified by Kaye, which match exactly with the yogatārās identified by Burgess [1].

Table 4.1: Identification of yogatārās by Burgess [1]

No.	Nakṣatra	Yogatārā* (conjunction star)	Ecliptic Longitude**	Ecliptic Latitude**
1	Aświnī	β Ari (Aries)	33° 58′	8° 29′ N
2	Bharaṇī	35 Ari (Aries)	46° 56′	11° 19′ N
3	Kṛttikā	η Tau (Taurus)	60° 00′	4° 03′ N
4	Rohiṇī	α Tau (Taurus)	69° 47′	5° 28′ S
5	Mṛgaśirā	λ Ori (Orion)	83° 42′	13° 22′ S
6	Ārdrā	α Ori (Orion)	88° 45′	16° 02′ S
7	Punarvasu	β Gem (Gemini)	113° 13′	6° 41′ N
8	Puṣya	δ Cnc (Cancer)	128° 43′	0° 05′ N
9	Āśleṣā	ε Hya (Hydra)	132° 21′	11° 06′ S
10	Maghā	α Leo (Leo)	149° 50′	0° 28′ N
11	Pūrvaphālgunī	δ Leo (Leo)	161° 19′	14° 20′ N
12	Uttaraphālgunī	β Leo (Leo)	171° 37′	12° 16′ N
13	Hasta	δ Crv (Corvus)	193° 27′	12° 12′ S
14	Citrā	α Vir (Virgo)	203° 50′	2° 03′ S
15	Swāti	α Boo (Virgo)	204° 14′	30° 44′ N
16	Viśākhā	ι Lib (Libra)	231° 00′	1°51′ S
17	Anurādhā	δ Sco (Scorpius)	242° 34′	1° 59′ S
18	Jyeṣṭhā	α Sco (Scorpius)	249° 46′	4° 34′ S
19	Mūla	λ Sco (Scorpius)	264° 35′	13° 47′ S
20	Pūrvāṣāḍhā	δ Sgr (Sagittarius)	274° 35′	6° 28′ S
21	Uttarāṣāḍhā	σ Sgr (Sagittarius)	282° 23′	3° 27′ S
22	Abhijit	α Lyr (Lyra)	285° 19′	61° 44′ N
23	Śravaṇa	α Aql (Aquila)	301° 47′	29° 18′ N
24	Dhaniṣṭhā	β Del (Delphinus)	316° 20′	31° 55′ N
25	Śatabhiṣaja	λ Aqr (Aquarius)	341° 35′	0° 23′ S
26	Pūrvabhādrapadā	α Peg (Pegasus)	353° 29′	19° 24′ N
27a	Uttara-bhādrapadā***	α And (Andromeda)	14° 19′	25° 41′ N
27b	Uttara-bhādrapadā***	γ Peg (Pegasus)	9° 09′	12° 36′ N
28	Revatī	ζ Psc (Pisces)	19° 53′	0° 13′ S

* As identified by Burgess [1]

** J2000.0 ecliptic coordinates based on Stellarium software.

*** For Uttara-bhādrapadā, longitude matches γ Pegasi, while latitude matches α Andromeda.

Table 4.2: Number of stars in nakṣatras

	Nakṣatra	Nakṣatra-Kalpa [2]	Śārdūla-karṇāvadāna [2]	Garga-saṃhitā [2]	Jain text*
1	Abhijit	1	3	3	3
2	Śravaṇa	3	3	3	3
3	Dhaniṣṭhā	5	4	4	5
4	Śatabhiṣaja	1	1	1	100
5	Pūrva-bhādrapadā	4	2	2	2
6	Uttara-bhādrapadā		2	2	2
7	Revatī	1	1	4	32
8	Aświnī	2	2	2	3
9	Bharaṇī	3	3	3	3
10	Kṛttikā	6	6	6	6
11	Rohiṇī	1	5	5	5
12	Mṛgaśirā	3	3	3	3
13	Ārdrā	1	1	1	1
14	Punarvasu	2	2	2	5
15	Puṣya	1	3	1	3
16	Āśleṣā	6	1	6	6
17	Maghā	6	5	6	7
18	Pūrva-phālgunī	4	2	2	2
19	Uttara-phālgunī		2	2	2
20	Hasta	5	5	5	5
21	Citrā	1	1	1	1
22	Swāti	1	1	1	1
23	Viśākhā	2	2	2	5
24	Anurādhā	4	4	4	4
25	Jyeṣṭhā	1	3	3	3
26	Mūla	7	7	6	11
27	Pūrvāṣāḍhā	8	4	4	4
28	Uttarāṣāḍhā		4	4	4

* Jambudwīpa Prajñapti 7.191

Jambudwīpa Prajñapti 7.192 gives the shapes and positions of nakṣatras relative to moon's path as shown in Table 4.3.

Table 4.3: Shape and position of nakṣatras in Jain astronomy according to Jambudwīpa Prajñapti 7.192

	Nakṣatra	Shape	Position
1	Abhijit	Head of cow	Always north
2	Śravaṇa	Rod with two baskets	Always north
3	Dhaniṣṭhā	Birdcage	Always north
4	Śatabhiṣaja	Collection of flowers	Always north
5	Pūrva-bhādrapadā	Half stepwell	Always north
6	Uttara-bhādrapadā	Half stepwell	Always north
7	Revatī	Boat	Always north
8	Aświnī	Horse shoulder	Always north
9	Bharaṇī	Female private part	Always north
10	Kṛttikā	Hairdresser's toolbox	North and south
11	Rohiṇī	Cart	North and south
12	Mṛgaśirā	Head of deer	Always south
13	Ārdrā	Drop of blood	Always south
14	Punarvasu	Balance	North and south
15	Puṣya	A type of earthen lamp	Always south
16	Āśleṣā	Flag	Always south
17	Maghā	Rampart	North and south
18	Pūrva-phālgunī	Half bed	Always north
19	Uttara-phālgunī	Half bed	Always north
20	Hasta	Hand	Always south
21	Citrā	A type of flower	North and south
22	Swāti	Nail	Always north
23	Viśākhā	Rope	North and south
24	Anurādhā	Single string of pearls	North and south
25	Jyeṣṭhā	Elephant's tusk	South boundary
26	Mūla	Scorpion's tail	Always south
27	Pūrvāṣāḍhā	Imprint of elephant's leg	South boundary

28	Uttarāṣāḍhā	Sitting lion	South boundary

The nakṣatra star groups identified by Kaye [3] are shown in Figures 4.1 to 4.10. Proper name or HIP, Bayer designation, Flamsteed designation, apparent magnitude, ecliptic longitude (J2000.0), and ecliptic latitude (J2000.0) of these stars are shown in Tables 4.4 to 4.31. Currently accepted yogatārās are shown in bold letters and numbers in each table. The data for J2000.0 ecliptic longitudes and latitudes were obtained using Stellarium software by setting the date to January 1, 2000 at 12:00 noon and noting the ecliptic longitudes and latitudes by selecting the specific stars. In each table, stars are numbered in the order of increasing longitude.

1. Abhijit nakṣatra

Abhijit nakṣatra is shown in Figure 4.1. It consists of three stars listed in Table 4.4. The yogatārā of Abhijit nakṣatra is identified as Vega, which is a bright star with magnitude 0.00.

2. Śravaṇa nakṣatra

Śravaṇa nakṣatra is shown in Figure 4.1. It consists of three stars listed in Table 4.5. The yogatārā of Śravaṇa nakṣatra is identified as Altair, which is a bright star with magnitude 0.75.

3. Dhaniṣṭhā nakṣatra

Dhaniṣṭhā nakṣatra is shown in Figure 4.1. It consists of four stars according to Hindu and Buddhist texts as shown in Table 4.2. Current identifications of these stars are listed in Table 4.6 and numbered 1 to 4. However, Jain text

Jambudwīpa Prajñapti says that the Dhaniṣṭhā nakṣatra has five stars. The fifth star in the Dhaniṣṭhā nakṣatra can be identified with ζ Del (4 Del) having apparent magnitude of 4.60, J2000.0 ecliptic longitude of 315° 46′ and J2000.0 ecliptic latitude of 32° 09′. It is listed as number 5 in Table 4.6. The yogatārā of Dhaniṣṭhā nakṣatra is currently identified as Rotanev, however, I have identified the yogatārā of Dhaniṣṭhā as Al Saib [4].

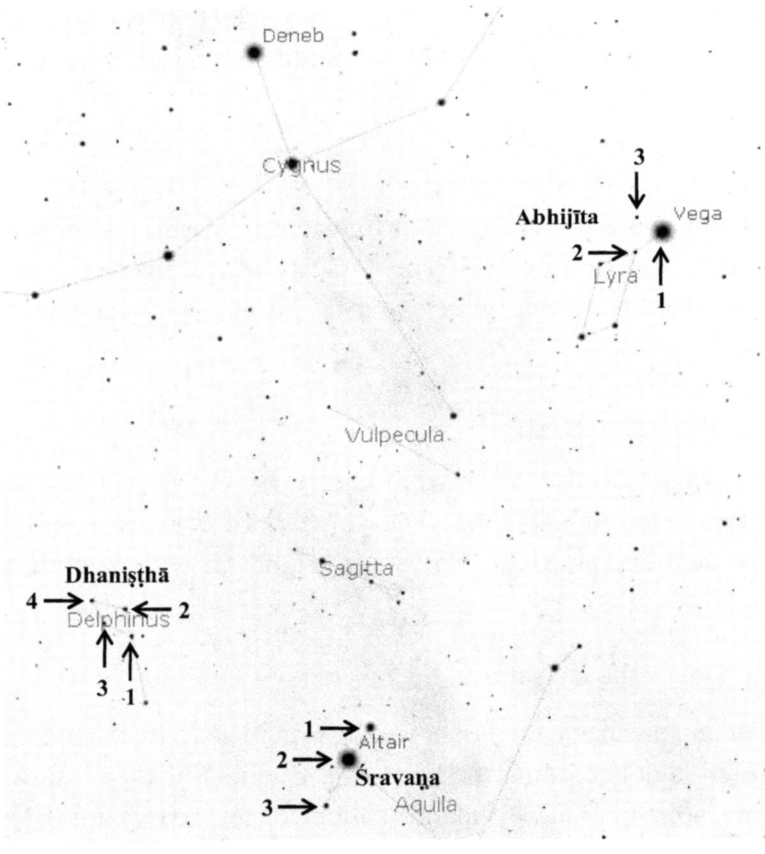

Figure 4.1: Abhijit, Śravaṇa, and Dhaniṣṭhā nakṣatras

Table 4.4: Abhijit nakṣatra

	Proper name	Bayer designation	Flamsteed designation	Apparent Magnitude	Ecliptic longitude	Ecliptic latitude
1.	**Vega**	**α Lyr**	**3 Lyr**	**0.00**	**285° 19′**	**61° 44′**
2.	Nasr Alwaki I	ζ1 Lyr	6 Lyr	4.30	288° 06′	60° 21′
3.	Double Double I	ε1 Lyr	4 Lyr	5.00	288° 38′	62° 24′

Table 4.5: Śravaṇa nakṣatra

	Proper name	Bayer designation	Flamsteed designation	Apparent Magnitude	Ecliptic longitude	Ecliptic latitude
1.	Tarazed	γ Aql	50 Aql	2.70	300° 56′	31° 15′
2.	**Altair**	**α Aql**	**53 Aql**	**0.75**	**301° 47′**	**29° 18′**
3.	Alshain	β Aql	60 Aql	3.70	302° 25′	26° 40′

Table 4.6: Dhaniṣṭhā nakṣatra

	Proper name	Bayer designation	Flamsteed designation	Apparent Magnitude	Ecliptic longitude	Ecliptic latitude
1.	**Rotanev**	**β Del**	**6 Del**	**4.10**	**316° 20′**	**31° 55′**
2.	Sualocin	α Del	9 Del	3.85	317° 23′	33° 01′
3.	Al Ukud	δ Del	11 Del	4.40	318° 07′	31° 57′
4.	Al Salib	γ2 Del	12 Del	4.25	319° 22′	32° 42′
5.	HIP 101589	ζ Del	4 Del	4.60	315° 46′	32° 09′

4. Śatabhiṣaja nakṣatra

Śatabhiṣaja nakṣatra is shown in Figure 4.2. It consists of a single star according to Hindu and Buddhist texts as shown in Table 4.2. Current identification of this star is Hydor as listed in Table 4.7. However, Jain text Jambudwīpa Prajñapti says that the Śatabhiṣaja nakṣatra has 100 stars and their positions are north of the trajectory of moon. Hydor is close to ecliptic and hence not north of the trajectory of moon. It is difficult to identify the group of stars belonging to Śatabhiṣaja nakṣatra according to Jain texts based on currently available information.

5. Pūrvabhādrapadā nakṣatra

Pūrvabhādrapadā nakṣatra is shown in Figure 4.2. It consists of two stars listed in Table 4.8. The yogatārā of Pūrvabhādrapadā nakṣatra is identified as Markab, which is a star with magnitude 2.45.

6. Uttarabhādrapadā nakṣatra

Uttarabhādrapadā nakṣatra is shown in Figure 4.2. It consists of two stars listed in Table 4.9. The yogatārā of Uttarabhādrapadā nakṣatra is identified as Alpheratz, which is a star with magnitude 2.05.

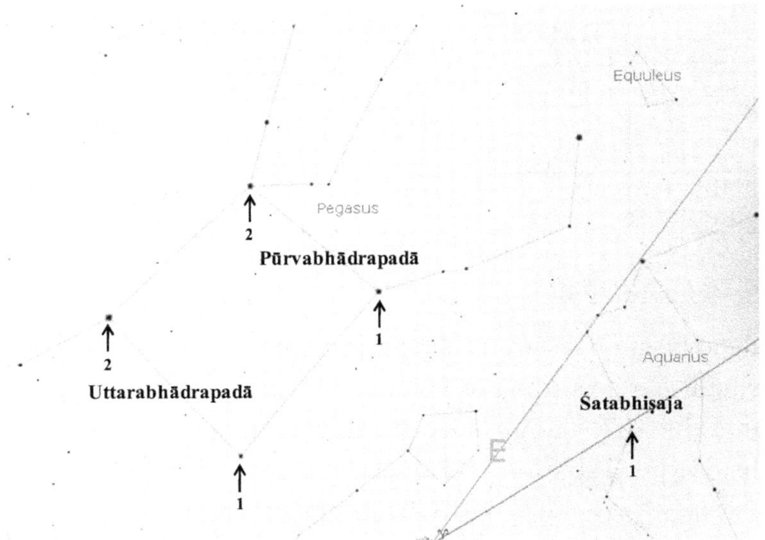

Figure 4.2: Śatabhiṣaja, Pūrvabhādrapadā, and Uttarabhādrapadā nakṣatras

Table 4.7: Śatabhiṣaja nakṣatra

	Proper name	Bayer designation	Flamsteed designation	Apparent Magnitude	Ecliptic longitude	Ecliptic latitude
1.	**Hydor**	**λ Aqr**	**73 Aqr**	**3.70**	**341° 35′**	**-0° 23′**

Table 4.8: Pūrvabhādrapadā nakṣatra

	Proper name	Bayer designation	Flamsteed designation	Apparent Magnitude	Ecliptic longitude	Ecliptic latitude
1.	**Markab**	**α Peg**	**54 Peg**	**2.45**	**353° 29′**	**19° 24′**
2.	Scheat	β Peg	53 Peg	2.40	359° 22′	31° 08′

Table 4.9: Uttarabhādrapadā nakṣatra

	Proper name	Bayer designation	Flamsteed designation	Apparent Magnitude	Ecliptic longitude	Ecliptic latitude
1.	Algenib	γ Peg	88 Peg	2.80	9° 09′	12° 36′
2.	**Alpheratz**	**α And** **δ Peg**	**21 And**	**2.05**	**14° 19′**	**25° 41′**

7. Revatī nakṣatra

Revatī nakṣatra is shown in Figure 4.3. It consists of a single star according to Hindu and Buddhist texts as shown in Table 4.2. Current identification of this star is Revati (Kuton II) as listed in Table 4.10. However, Jain text Jambudwīpa Prajñapti says that the Revatī nakṣatra has 32 stars and their positions are north of the trajectory of moon. Revati (Kuton II) is close to ecliptic and hence not north of the trajectory of moon. It is difficult to identify the group of stars belonging to Revatī nakṣatra according to Jain texts based on currently available information.

8. Aświnī nakṣatra

Aświnī nakṣatra is shown in Figure 4.3. It consists of two stars according to Hindu and Buddhist texts as shown in

Table 4.2. Current identification of these stars is shown in Figure 4.3 and numbered 1 and 2. However, Jain text Jambudwīpa Prajñapti says that the Aświnī nakṣatra has 3 stars. This third star is Hamal and is listed in Table 4.11 as number 3. The yogatārā of Aświnī nakṣatra is currently identified as Sheraton, however, I have identified the yogatārā of Aświnī as Hamal [4]. This is of critical importance in determining the chronology of Indian history.

9. Bharaṇī nakṣatra

Bharaṇī nakṣatra is shown in Figure 4.3. It consists of three stars listed in Table 4.12. The yogatārā of Bharaṇī nakṣatra is currently identified as Barani II, however, I have identified the yogatārā of Bharaṇī as Bharani [4].

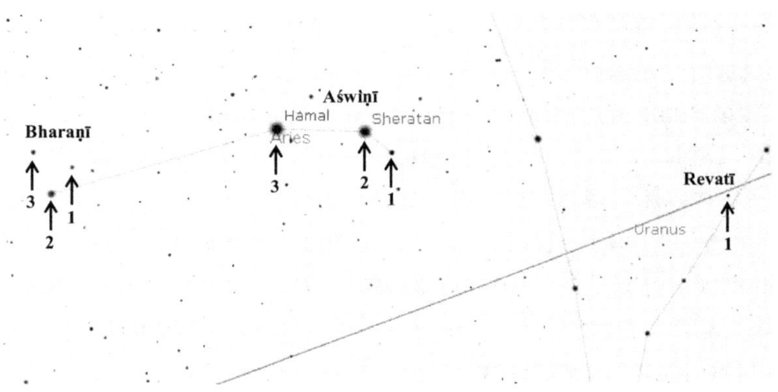

Figure 4.3: Revatī, Aświnī, and Bharaṇī nakṣatras

Table 4.10: Revatī nakṣatra

	Proper name	Bayer designation	Flamsteed designation	Apparent Magnitude	Ecliptic longitude	Ecliptic latitude
1.	**Revati (Kuton II)**	**ζ Psc A**	**86 Psc A**	**5.20**	**19° 53′**	**-0° 13′**

Table 4.11: Aświnī nakṣatra

	Proper name	Bayer designation	Flamsteed designation	Apparent Magnitude	Ecliptic longitude	Ecliptic latitude
1.	Mesarthim	γ1 Ari	5 Ari	4.50	33° 11′	7° 10′
2.	**Sheratan**	**β Ari**	**6 Ari**	**2.60**	**33° 58′**	**8° 29′**
3.	Hamal	α Ari	13 Ari	2.00	37° 40′	9° 58′

Table 4.12: Bharaṇī nakṣatra

	Proper name	Bayer designation	Flamsteed designation	Apparent Magnitude	Ecliptic longitude	Ecliptic latitude
1.	**Barani II**		**35 Ari**	**4.65**	**46° 56′**	**11° 19′**
2.	Bharani		41 Ari	3.60	48° 12′	10° 27′
3.	Barani III		39 Ari	4.50	48° 22′	12° 29′

10. Kṛttikā nakṣatra

Kṛttikā nakṣatra is shown in Figure 4.4. It consists of six stars listed in Table 4.13. The yogatārā of Kṛttikā nakṣatra is identified as Alcyone, which is a star with magnitude 2.85.

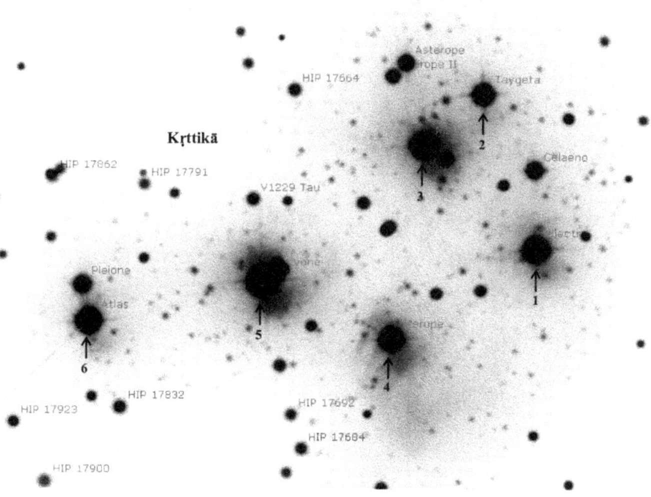

Figure 4.4: Kṛttikā nakṣatra

Table 4.13: Kṛttikā nakṣatra

	Proper name	Bayer designation	Flamsteed designation	Apparent Magnitude	Ecliptic longitude	Ecliptic latitude
1.	Electra		17 Tau	3.70	59° 25′	4° 11′
2.	Taygeta	q Tau	19 Tau	4.30	59° 34′	4° 31′
3.	Maia		20 Tau	3.85	59° 41′	4° 23′
4.	Merope		23 Tau	4.10	59° 42′	3° 57′
5.	**Alcyone**	**η Tau**	**25 Tau**	**2.85**	**60° 00′**	**4° 03′**
6.	Atlas		27 Tau	3.60	60° 21′	3° 55′

11. Rohiṇī nakṣatra

Rohiṇī nakṣatra is shown in Figure 4.5. It consists of five stars listed in Table 4.14. The yogatārā of Rohiṇī nakṣatra is identified as Aldebaran, which is a bright star with magnitude 0.85.

12. Mṛgaśirā nakṣatra

Mṛgaśirā nakṣatra is shown in Figure 4.5. It consists of three stars listed in Table 4.15. The yogatārā of Mṛgaśirā nakṣatra is identified as Meissa, which is a star with magnitude 3.50.

13. Ārdrā nakṣatra

Ārdrā nakṣatra is shown in Figure 4.5. It consists of a single star listed in Table 4.16. The yogatārā of Ārdrā nakṣatra is identified as Betelgeuse, which is a bright star with magnitude 0.45.

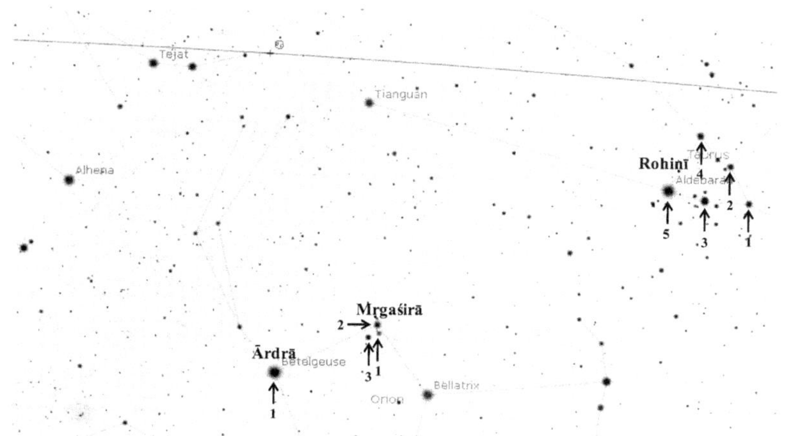

Figure 4.5: Rohiṇī, Mṛgaśirā, and Ārdrā nakṣatras

Table 4.14: Rohiṇī nakṣatra

	Proper name	Bayer designation	Flamsteed designation	Apparent Magnitude	Ecliptic longitude	Ecliptic latitude
1.	Hyadum I	γ Tau	54 Tau	3.65	65° 48′	-5° 44′
2.	Hyadum II	δ1 Tau	61 Tau	3.75	66° 52′	-3° 58′
3.	Hyadum IV	θ2 Tau	78 Tau	3.40	67° 58′	-5° 50′
4.	Ain	ε Tau	74 Tau	3.50	68° 28′	-2° 34′
5.	**Aldebaran**	**α Tau**	**87 Tau**	**0.85**	**69° 47′**	**-5° 28′**

Table 4.15: Mṛgaśirā nakṣatra

	Proper name/HIP	Bayer designation	Flamsteed designation	Apparent Magnitude	Ecliptic longitude	Ecliptic latitude
1.	Heka	ϕ1 Ori	37 Ori	4.35	83° 36′	-13° 49′
2.	**Meissa**	**λ Ori**	**39 Ori**	**3.50**	**83° 42′**	**-13° 22′**
3.	HIP 26366	ϕ2 Ori	40 Ori	4.05	84° 08′	-14° 02′

Table 4.16: Ārdrā nakṣatra

	Proper name	Bayer designation	Flamsteed designation	Apparent Magnitude	Ecliptic longitude	Ecliptic latitude
1.	**Betelgeuse**	**α Ori**	**58 Ori**	**0.45**	**88° 45′**	**-16° 02′**

14. Punarvasu nakṣatra

Punarvasu nakṣatra is shown in Figure 4.6. It consists of two stars according to Hindu and Buddhist texts as shown in Table 4.2. Current identification of these stars is shown in Table 4.17. However, Jain text Jambudwīpa Prajñapti says that the Punarvasu nakṣatra has 5 stars and they are located north as well as south of moon's trajectory. Currently identified stars are located north of moon's trajectory. There are other stars in the vicinity that qualify to be listed as belonging to Punarvasu nakṣatra, but it is difficult to identify them unambiguously. The yogatārā of Punarvasu nakṣatra is identified as Pollux, which is a star with magnitude 1.15.

15. Puṣya nakṣatra

Puṣya nakṣatra is shown in Figure 4.6. It consists of a single star according to Hindu texts and three stars according to Jain and Buddhist texts as shown in Table 4.2. Current identification of these three stars is shown in Table 4.18. According to Jambudwīpa Prajñapti these three stars are located south of the trajectory of moon. Currently identified stars are located close to ecliptic and hence are not located south of moon's trajectory. It is difficult to identify the stars Jain astronomers had in mind based on the available information. The yogatārā of Puṣya nakṣatra is identified as Asellus Australis, which is a star with magnitude 3.90.

16. Āśleṣā nakṣatra

Āśleṣā nakṣatra is shown in Figure 4.6. It consists of six stars according to Hindu and Jain texts. Kaye [3] has listed only five stars as shown in Table 4.19 and numbered 1 to 5. The sixth star can be identified as Minazal V, which is in the vicinity and listed as number 6 in Table 4.19. The yogatārā of Āśleṣā nakṣatra is identified as Minazal III, which is a star with magnitude 3.40.

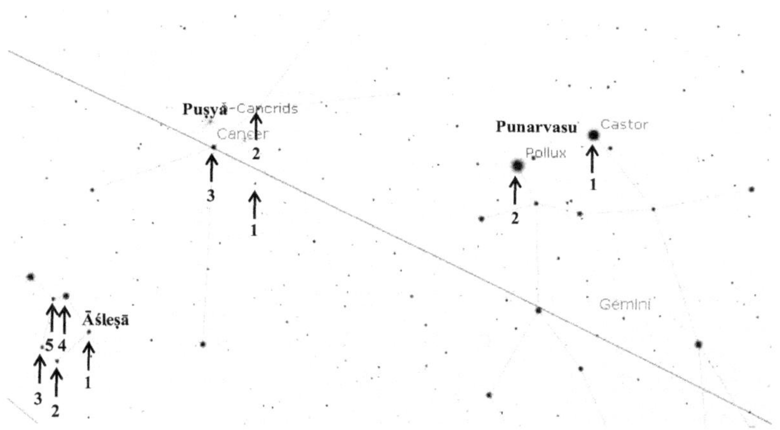

Figure 4.6: Punarvasu, Puṣya, and Āśleṣā nakṣatras

Table 4.17: Punarvasu nakṣatra

	Proper name	Bayer designation	Flamsteed designation	Apparent Magnitude	Ecliptic longitude	Ecliptic latitude
1.	Castor	α Gem	66 Gem	1.90	110° 14′	10° 06′
2.	**Pollux**	**β Gem**	**78 Gem**	**1.15**	**113° 13′**	**6° 41′**

Table 4.18: Puṣya nakṣatra

	Proper name/HIP	Bayer designation	Flamsteed designation	Apparent Magnitude	Ecliptic longitude	Ecliptic latitude
1.	HIP 41822	θ Cnc	31 Cnc	5.30	125° 44′	-0° 46′
2.	Asellus Borealis	γ Cnc	43 Cnc	4.65	127° 32′	3° 11′
3.	**Asellus Australis**	**δ Cnc**	**47 Cnc**	**3.90**	**128° 43′**	**0° 05′**

Table 4.19: Āśleṣā nakṣatra

	Proper name/HIP	Bayer designation	Flamsteed designation	Apparent Mag.	Ecliptic longitude	Ecliptic latitude
1.	Minazal I	δ Hya	4 Hya	4.10	130° 18′	-12° 24′
2.	Minkalshuja	σ Hya	5 Hya	4.45	131° 13′	-14° 36′
3.	Minazal II	η Hya	7 Hya	4.30	132° 18′	-14° 15′
4.	**Minazal III**	**ε Hya**	**11 Hya**	**3.40**	**132° 21′**	**-11° 06′**
5.	Minazal IV	ρ Hya	13 Hya	4.35	132° 55′	-11° 33′
6.	Minazal V	ζ Hya	16 Hya	3.10	134° 35′	-10° 58′

17. Maghā nakṣatra

Maghā nakṣatra consists of six stars according to Hindu texts. Current identification of these six stars is shown in Figure 4.7 and listed in Table 4.20. Jain texts show seven stars, but it is difficult to identify the seventh star Jain astronomers had in mind based on the available information. The yogatārā of Maghā nakṣatra is identified as Regulus, which is a bright star with magnitude 1.35.

18. Pūrva-phālgunī nakṣatra

Pūrva-phālgunī nakṣatra is shown in Figure 4.7. It consists of two stars listed in Table 4.21. The yogatārā of Pūrva-phālgunī nakṣatra is identified as Zosma, which is a star with magnitude 2.55.

19. Uttara-phālgunī nakṣatra

Uttara-phālgunī nakṣatra is shown in Figure 4.7. It consists of two stars listed in Table 4.22. The yogatārā of Uttara-phālgunī nakṣatra is identified as Denebola, which is a star with magnitude 2.10.

20. Hasta nakṣatra

Hasta nakṣatra is shown in Figure 4.7. It consists of five stars listed in Table 4.23. The yogatārā of Hasta nakṣatra is currently identified as Algorab, however, I have identified the yogatārā of Hasta as Gienah [4].

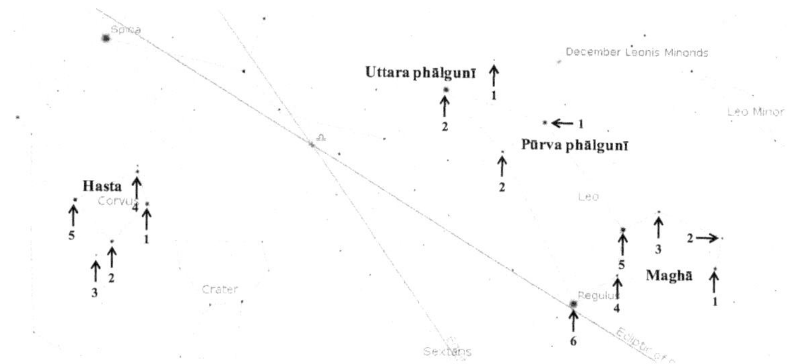

Figure 4.7: Maghā, Pūrva-phālgunī, Uttara-phālgunī, and Hasta nakṣatras

Table 4.20: Maghā nakṣatra

	Proper name	Bayer designation	Flamsteed designation	Apparent Magnitude	Ecliptic longitude	Ecliptic latitude
1.	Algenubi	ε Leo	17 Leo	2.95	140° 42′	9° 43′
2.	Rasalas	μ Leo	24 Leo	3.85	141° 26′	12° 21′
3.	Adhafera	ζ Leo	36 Leo	3.40	147° 34′	11° 52′
4.	Al Jabhah	η Leo	30 Leo	3.45	147° 54′	4° 52′
5.	Algieba	γ1 Leo	41 Leo	2.20	149° 37′	8° 49′
6.	**Regulus**	**α Leo**	**32 Leo**	**1.35**	**149° 50′**	**0° 28′**

Table 4.21: Pūrva-phālgunī nakṣatra

	Proper name	Bayer designation	Flamsteed designation	Apparent Magnitude	Ecliptic longitude	Ecliptic latitude
1.	**Zosma**	**δ Leo**	**68 Leo**	**2.55**	**161° 19′**	**14° 20′**
2.	Chertan	θ Leo	70 Leo	3.30	163° 25′	9° 40′

Table 4.22: Uttara-phālgunī nakṣatra

	Proper name/HIP	Bayer designation	Flamsteed designation	Apparent Magnitude	Ecliptic longitude	Ecliptic latitude
1.	HIP 57565		93 Leo	4.50	168° 58′	17° 19′
2.	**Denebola**	**β Leo**	**94 Leo**	**2.10**	**171° 37′**	**12° 16′**

Table 4.23: Hasta nakṣatra

	Proper name	Bayer designation	Flamsteed designation	Apparent Magnitude	Ecliptic longitude	Ecliptic latitude
1.	Gienah	γ Crv	4 Crv	2.55	190° 44′	-14° 30′
2.	Minkar	ε Crv	2 Crv	3.00	191° 40′	-19° 40′
3.	Alchiba	α Crv	1 Crv	4.00	192° 15′	-21° 45′
4.	**Algorab**	**δ Crv**	**7 Crv**	**2.90**	**193° 27′**	**-12° 12′**
5.	Kraz	β Crv	9 Crv	2.65	197° 22′	-18° 03′

21. Citrā nakṣatra

Citrā nakṣatra is shown in Figure 4.8. It consists of a single star as listed in Table 4.24. The yogatārā of Citrā nakṣatra is identified as Spica, which is a bright star with magnitude 0.95.

22. Swāti nakṣatra

Swāti nakṣatra is shown in Figure 4.8. It consists of a single star as listed in Table 4.25. The yogatārā of Swāti nakṣatra is currently identified as Arcturus, however, I have identified the yogatārā of Swāti as Alphecca [4].

23. Viśākhā nakṣatra

Viśākhā nakṣatra is shown in Figure 4.8. It consists of two stars according to Hindu and Buddhist texts, but five stars according to Jain texts. Kaye [3] has listed four stars as shown in Table 4.26. The yogatārā of Viśākhā nakṣatra is identified as ι1 Lib, which is a dim star with magnitude 4.5.

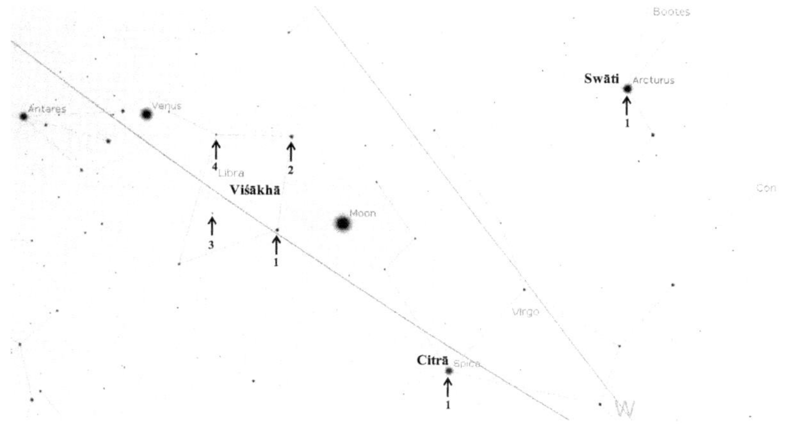

Figure 4.8: Citrā, Swāti and Viśākhā nakṣatras

Table 4.24: Citrā nakṣatra

	Proper name	Bayer designation	Flamsteed designation	Apparent Magnitude	Ecliptic longitude	Ecliptic latitude
1.	**Spica**	**α Vir**	**67 Vir**	**0.95**	**203° 50′**	**-2° 03′**

Table 4.25: Swāti nakṣatra

	Proper name	Bayer designation	Flamsteed designation	Apparent Magnitude	Ecliptic longitude	Ecliptic latitude
1.	**Arcturus**	**α Boo**	**16 Boo**	**0.15**	**204° 14′**	**30° 43′**

Table 4.26: Viśākhā nakṣatra

	Proper name/HIP	Bayer designation	Flamsteed designation	Apparent Magnitude	Ecliptic longitude	Ecliptic latitude
1.	Zuben-elgenubi II	α2 Lib	9 Lib	2.75	225° 05′	0° 20′
2.	Zuben-eschamali	β Lib	27 Lib	2.60	229° 22′	8° 30′
3.	**HIP 74392**	**ι1 Lib**	**24 Lib**	**4.50**	**231° 00′**	**-1° 51′**
4.	Zuben Elakrab	γ Lib	38 Lib	3.90	235° 08′	4° 23′

24. Anurādhā nakṣatra

Anurādhā nakṣatra is shown in Figure 4.9. It consists of four stars in all texts. Kaye [3] has listed only three stars, which are shown in Table 4.27 and numbered 1 to 3. According to Jain texts, its shape is that of a single string of pearls. Based on this description, fourth star can be identified as Iolil (ρ Sco). Its apparent magnitude and J2000.0 ecliptic coordinates are listed in Table 4.27 in last row. The yogatārā of Anurādhā nakṣatra is identified as Dschubba, which is the brightest star in the group with magnitude 2.35.

25. Jyeṣṭhā nakṣatra

Jyeṣṭhā nakṣatra is shown in Figure 4.9. It consists of three stars in majority of texts. Kaye [3] has listed three stars, which are shown in Table 4.28. The yogatārā of Jyeṣṭhā nakṣatra is identified as Antares, which is a bright star with magnitude 1.05.

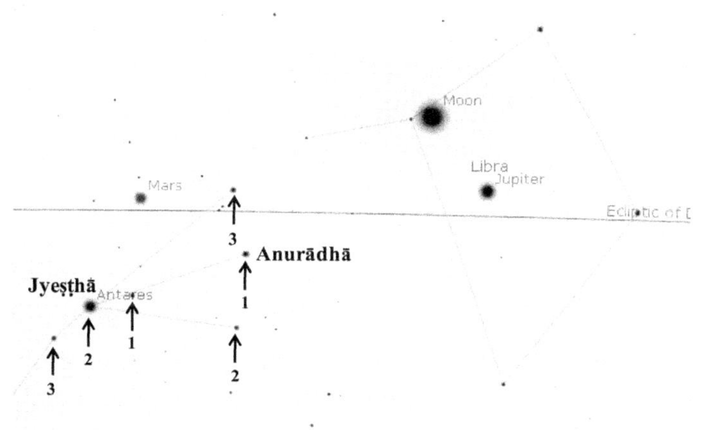

Figure 4.9: Anurādhā, and Jyeṣṭhā nakṣatras

Table 4.27: Anurādhā nakṣatra

	Proper name	Bayer designation	Flamsteed designation	Apparent Magnitude	Ecliptic longitude	Ecliptic latitude
1.	**Dschubba**	**δ Sco**	**7 Sco**	**2.35**	**242° 34′**	**-1° 59′**
2.	Fang	π Sco	6 Sco	2.85	242° 56′	-5° 29′
3.	Acrab	β1 Sco	8 Sco	2.60	243° 11′	1° 00′
4.	Iolil	ρ Sco	5 Sco	3.85	243° 09′	-8° 36′

Table 4.28: Jyeṣṭhā nakṣatra

	Proper name	Bayer designation	Flamsteed designation	Apparent Magnitude	Ecliptic longitude	Ecliptic latitude
1.	Alniyat	σ Sco	20 Sco	3.05	247° 48′	-4° 02′
2.	**Antares**	**α Sco**	**21 Sco**	**1.05**	**249° 46′**	**-4° 34′**
3.	Alniyat II	τ Sco	23 Sco	2.80	251° 27′	-6° 07′

26. Mūla nakṣatra

Mūla nakṣatra is shown in Figure 4.10. It consists of six, seven, or 11 stars according to texts. Kaye [3] has listed seven stars, which are shown in Table 4.29. Jain texts mention eleven stars. This means that Jain astronomers considered additional stars in the vicinity to belong to Mūla nakṣatra. The yogatārā of Mūla nakṣatra is identified as Shaula, which is a star with magnitude 1.60.

27. Pūrvāṣāḍhā nakṣatra

Pūrvāṣāḍhā nakṣatra is shown in Figure 4.10. It consists of four stars in all texts. Kaye [3] has listed only two stars, which are shown in Table 4.30. The yogatārā of Pūrvāṣāḍhā nakṣatra is identified as Kaus Media, which is a star with magnitude 2.70.

28. Uttarāṣāḍhā nakṣatra

Uttarāṣāḍhā nakṣatra is shown in Figure 4.10. It consists of four stars in all texts. Kaye [3] has listed only two stars, which are shown in Table 4.31. The yogatārā of Uttarāṣāḍhā nakṣatra is identified as Nunki, which is a star with magnitude 2.05.

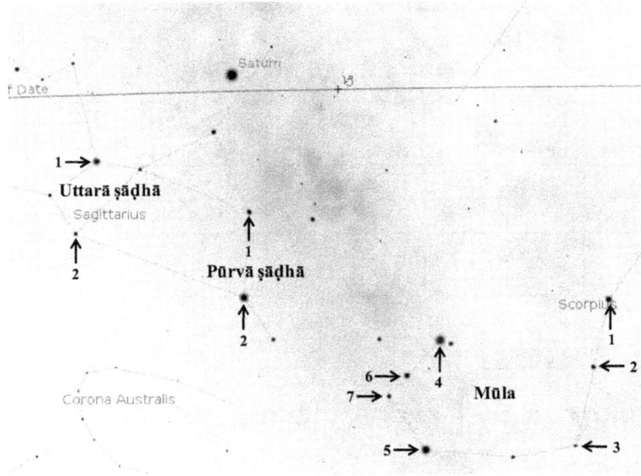

Figure 4.10: Mūla, Pūrvāṣāḍhā, and Uttarāṣāḍhā nakṣatras

Table 4.29: Mūla nakṣatra

	Proper name/HIP	Bayer designation	Flamsteed designation	Apparent Magnitude	Ecliptic longitude	Ecliptic latitude
1.	HIP 82396	ε Sco	26 Sco	2.25	255° 20′	-11° 44′
2.	Tali al Shaulah I	μ1 Sco		3.00	256° 09′	-15° 25′
3.	HIP 82729	ζ2 Sco		3.60	257° 14′	-19° 39′
4.	**Shaula**	**λ Sco**	**35 Sco**	**1.60**	**264° 35′**	**-13° 47′**
5.	Sargas	θ Sco		1.85	265° 36′	-19° 39′
6.	Mula	κ Sco		2.35	266° 28′	-15° 39′
7.	Girtab	ι1 Sco		2.95	267° 31′	-16° 43′

Table 4.30: Pūrvāṣāḍhā nakṣatra

	Proper name/HIP	Bayer designation	Flamsteed designation	Apparent Magnitude	Ecliptic longitude	Ecliptic latitude
1.	**Kaus Media**	**δ Sgr**	**19 Sgr**	**2.70**	**274° 35′**	**-6° 28′**
2.	Kaus Australis	ε Sgr	20 Sgr	1.75	275° 05′	-11° 03′

Table 4.31: Uttarāṣāḍhā nakṣatra

	Proper name/HIP	Bayer designation	Flamsteed designation	Apparent Magnitude	Ecliptic longitude	Ecliptic latitude
1.	**Nunki**	**σ Sgr**	**34 Sgr**	**2.05**	**282° 23′**	**-3° 27′**
2.	Ascella	ζ Sgr	38 Sgr	3.25	283° 38′	-7° 11′

With the tabulation of currently accepted identifications of nakṣatra star groups and yogatārās, we are in a position to estimate the date when the astronomical observations described in Jain texts were made.

Notes

1. Burgess (1860).
2. Pingree and Morrissey (1989).
3. Kaye (1924).
4. Roy (2020).

"The stars are the land-marks of the universe."
– Sir John Frederick William Herschel

5. Zero Point of Jain Astronomy

Jain astronomers kept a very meticulous record of the positions of sun and moon in the background of nakṣatras during the course of the year. There are four very important dates in a year from the point of astronomy; vernal equinox, summer solstice, autumnal equinox, and winter solstice. In western calendar, these dates mark the beginning of spring, summer, fall, and winter respectively. Jain text Triloka Prajñapti provides detailed information about the position of moon during solstices and equinoxes as shown in Tables 5.1 to 5.4. The position of sun has been obtained by noting that on full moon day sun is diagonally opposite the position of moon and on no moon day the sun and moon are in same naksatra. The position of moon was in Swāti on Kārttika full moon day on autumnal equinox according to Triloka Prajñapti. This will mean that sun was diagonally opposite in Aświnī on autumnal equinox. Similarly, the position of moon was in Aświnī on Vaiśākha full moon day on vernal equinox according to Triloka Prajñapti. This will mean that sun was diagonally opposite in Swāti on vernal equinox.

Table 5.1: The position of sun and moon at summer solstice [1]

Year	Month and Tithi	Sun's nakṣatra	Moon's nakṣatra
1	Śrāvaṇa dark 1st	Puṣya	Abhijit
2	Śrāvaṇa dark 13th	Puṣya	Mṛgaśirā
3	Śrāvaṇa bright 10th	Puṣya	Viśākhā
4	Śrāvaṇa dark 7th	Puṣya	Revatī
5	Śrāvaṇa bright 4th	Puṣya	Pūrva-phālgunī

Table 5.2: The position of sun and moon at autumnal equinox [2]

Year	Month and Tithi	Sun's nakṣatra	Moon's nakṣatra
1	Kārttika dark 3rd	Swāti	Rohiṇī
2	Kārttika full moon	Swāti	Swāti
3	Kārttika bright 12th	Swāti	Uttara-bhādrapadā
4	Kārttika dark 9th	Swāti	Maghā
5	Kārttika bright 6th	Swāti	Uttarā-ṣāḍhā

Table 5.3: The position of sun and moon at winter solstice [3]

Year	Month and Tithi	Sun's nakṣatra	Moon's nakṣatra
1	Māgha dark 7th	Abhijit	Hasta
2	Māgha bright 4th	Abhijit	Śatabhisaja
3	Māgha dark 1st	Abhijit	Puṣya
4	Māgha dark 13th	Abhijit	Mūla
5	Māgha bright 10th	Abhijit	Kṛttikā

Table 5.4: The position of sun and moon at vernal equinox [2]

Year	Month and Tithi	Sun's nakṣatra	Moon's nakṣatra
1	Vaiśākha dark 9th	Aświnī	Dhaniṣṭhā
2	Vaiśākha bright 6th	Aświnī	Punarvasu
3	Vaiśākha dark 3rd	Aświnī	Anuradhā
4	Vaiśākha full moon	Aświnī	Aświnī
5	Vaiśākha bright 12th	Aświnī	Uttara-phālgunī

Both of these observations are inconsistent with the information on the positions of sun during solstices. Fortunately, it is easy to fix these errors and make the data consistent. For this purpose, the data given in Triloka Prajñapti on equinoxes is presented in Table 5.5. It can be seen that equinoxes were separated by 12 fortnights (six synodic months) and six days. If we count 12 fortnights and six days from the second equinox, we get no moon day instead of full moon day. Similarly, if we count 12 fortnights and six days from the seventh equinox, we get no moon day instead of full moon day. Thus both of these dates were no moon days instead of full moon days. Since sun and moon are in same naksatra on no moon day, sun was in Aświnī on vernal equinox and Swāti on autumnal equinox as shown in Tables 5.2 and 5.4.

The information presented above is shown in Figure 5.1 and can be used to estimate the date when these observations were made. It is customary to measure the ecliptic longitude from vernal equinox and accordingly the ecliptic longitudes of vernal equinox, summer solstice, autumnal equinox and winter solstice are 0°, 90°, 180°, and 270° respectively as shown in Figure 5.1.

5.1 Ecliptic coordinates

Ecliptic coordinates measure the coordinates from and along the ecliptic, which is a great circle on the celestial sphere representing the sun's apparent path during a year. The poles of the ecliptic are called North Ecliptic Pole (NEP) and South Ecliptic Pole (SEP).

Table 5.5: Period between equinoxes [2]

Year	Equinox	Type of equinox	Fortnights past	Month	Tithi
1	1	Fall	6	Kārttika	dark 3rd
1	2	Spring	18	Vaiśākha	dark 9th
2	3	Fall	31	Kārttika	full moon
2	4	Spring	43	Vaiśākha	bright 6th
3	5	Fall	55	Kārttika	white 12th
3	6	Spring	68	Vaiśākha	dark 3rd
4	7	Fall	80	Kārttika	dark 9th
4	8	Spring	93	Vaiśākha	full moon
5	9	Fall	105	Kārttika	bright 6th
5	10	Spring	117	Vaiśākha	bright 12th

Ecliptic coordinates are specified by providing ecliptic latitude and ecliptic longitude. Figure 5.2 illustrates the ecliptic coordinate system. In this picture K is the North Ecliptic Pole (NEP), ♈ is the first point of Aries, S is the location of a star, and K′ is the South Ecliptic Pole (SEP). Ecliptic latitude of the star is given by SA and the ecliptic longitude of the star is given by ♈A. In ecliptic coordinate system, ecliptic latitude is determined by measuring the angular distance from ecliptic to the star along the great circle passing through the star and the North Ecliptic Pole. Ecliptic longitude is determined by measuring the angular distance along the ecliptic from the first point of Aries to the intersection of the ecliptic and the great circle passing through the star and and the North Ecliptic Pole.

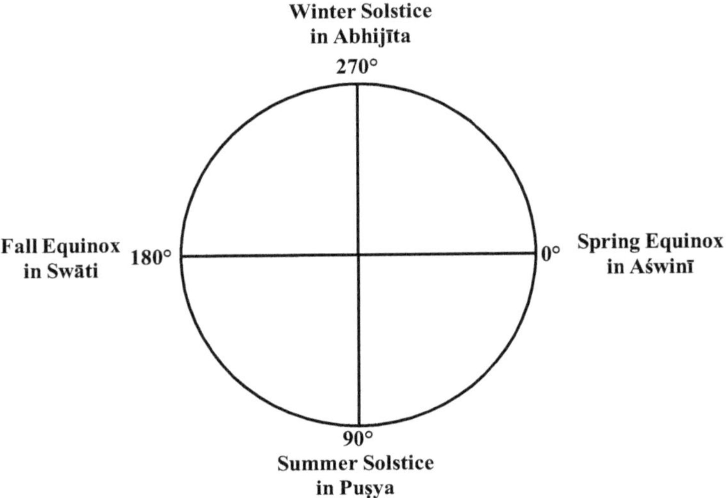

Figure 5.1: The position of sun during solstices and equinoxes in Jain astronomy

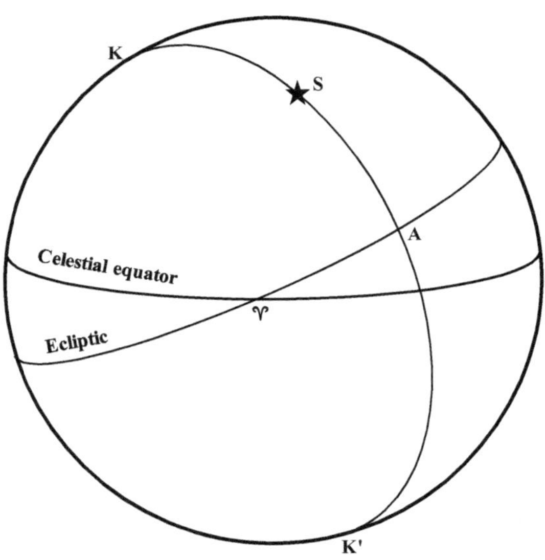

Figure 5.2: Illustration of the ecliptic coordinate system

The zero point of ecliptic longitude is called the First Point of Aries, which is the position of vernal equinox on the ecliptic. As this point keeps changing due to precession, ecliptic longitudes are specified with the associated year. Currently, it is customary to specify the ecliptic coordinates for year 2000 called J2000 coordinates. Modern astronomy software allows us to find the coordinates of any star in past 5,000 years or more.

5.2 The yogatārās at solstices and equinoxes

As shown in Table 5.3 and Figure 5.1, the sun was in Abhijit nakṣatra during winter solstice according to Jain astronomical texts. One way to estimate the time when this observation was made is to find when the ecliptic longitude of the yogatārā of Abhijit nakṣatra was 270°. The currently accepted yogatārā of Abhijit nakṣatra is star Vega (α Lyr) as described in Chapter 4. Using Stellarium software, it was found by trial and error that the star Vega had an ecliptic longitude of 270° in 901 CE as shown in Figure 5.3. This date is obviously too late. Currently accepted dates of Jain astronomical texts are 4th or 3rd century BCE [4]. This seems to be based on the yogatārā of Śravaṇa nakṣatra being at winter solstice. Since Abhijit nakṣatra has a short span, it was combined with Śravaṇa nakṣatra for observational purpose. The currently accepted yogatārā of Śravaṇa nakṣatra is star Altair (α Aql) as described in Chapter 4. Using Stellarium software, it was found by trial and error that the star Altair had an ecliptic longitude of 270° in 262 BCE as shown in Figure 5.4. We should note that since there was no zero CE, astronomical date of -261 is equivalent to 262 BCE.

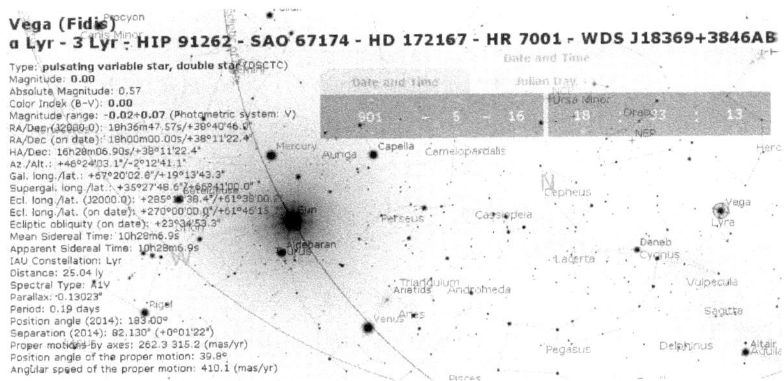

Figure 5.3: The yogatārā of Abhijit nakṣatra on winter solstice

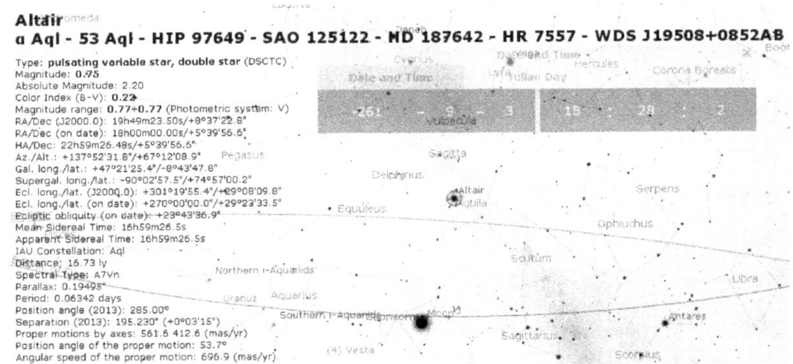

Figure 5.4: The yogatārā of Śravaṇa nakṣatra on winter solstice

Since Jain astronomical texts describe the sun being in Abhijit nakṣatra on winter solstice, and not in Śravaṇa nakṣatra, this date is not very convincing. Also, as described in Chapter 4, the ecliptic latitude of the yogatārā of Abhijit, Vega (α Lyr), is 61° 44′ and that of Śravaṇa, Altair (α Aql), is 29° 18′. Since the yogatārās of Śravaṇa and Abhijit are far away from ecliptic, it is plausible that the ecliptic longitudes of these yogatārās fall outside the boundaries of their respective nakṣatras.

Thus, the time of Jain astronomical observations determined from the ecliptic longitudes of the yogatārās of Śravaṇa and Abhijit may not be accurate. To get a better estimate, we need to analyze the available information in greater detail. As shown in Figure 5.1, the position of sun was in Aświnī nakṣatra during vernal equinox, in Puṣya nakṣatra during summer solstice, and in Swāti nakṣatra during autumnal equinox. Currently the accepted yogatārā of Aświnī nakṣatra is Sheraton (β Ari). The star Sheraton was at vernal equinox in 446 BCE as shown in Figure 5.5. However, after a detailed analysis of the coordinates of yogatārās given in Sūrya Siddhānta, author has proposed that the yogatārā of Aświnī is Hamal (α Ari) [5]. Also as shown in Table 4.2, while Hindu and Buddhist texts describe number of stars in Aświnī nakṣatra as two, Jain texts describe the number of stars in Aświnī nakṣatra as three. Currently, the stars belonging to Aświnī nakṣatra are identified as Sheraton (β Ari) and Mesarthim (γ Ari). Author has proposed that these two stars should be Hamal (α Ari) and Sheraton (β Ari) [5].

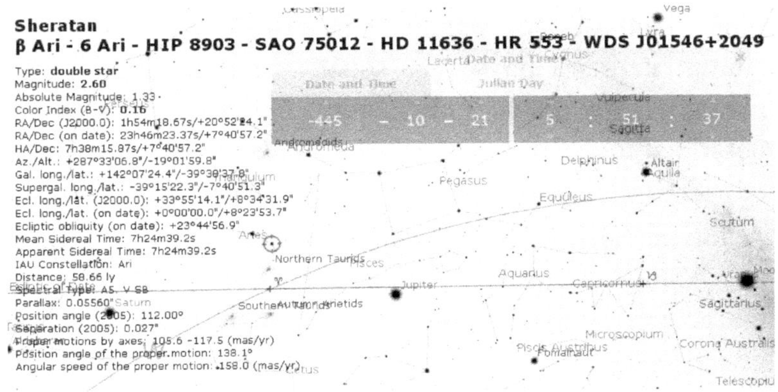

Figure 5.5: The currently accepted yogatārā of Aświnī nakṣatra on vernal equinox

The stars belonging to Aświnī nakṣatra according to Jain astronomy are Hamal (α Ari), Sheraton (β Ari), and Mesarthim (γ Ari). Since, Hamal (α Ari) is a much brighter star than Sheraton (β Ari), the yogatārā of Aświnī nakṣatra according to Jain astronomy is Hamal (α Ari). The star Hamal was at vernal equinox in 709 BCE as shown in Figure 5.6.

The currently accepted yogatārā of Puṣya nakṣatra is star Asellus Australis (δ Cnc) as described in Chapter 4. The star Asellus Australis was at summer solstice in 787 BCE as shown in Figure 5.7.

The currently accepted yogatārā of Swāti nakṣatra is star Arcturus (α Boo) as described in Chapter 4. The star Arcturus was at autumnal equinox in 265 CE as shown in Figure 5.8.

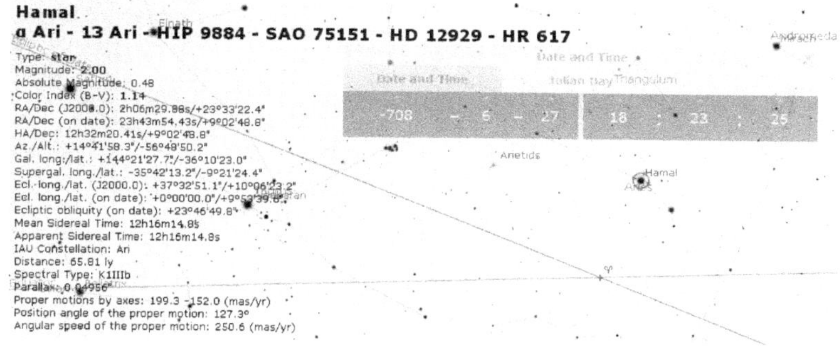

Figure 5.6: The proposed yogatārā of Aświnī nakṣatra on vernal equinox

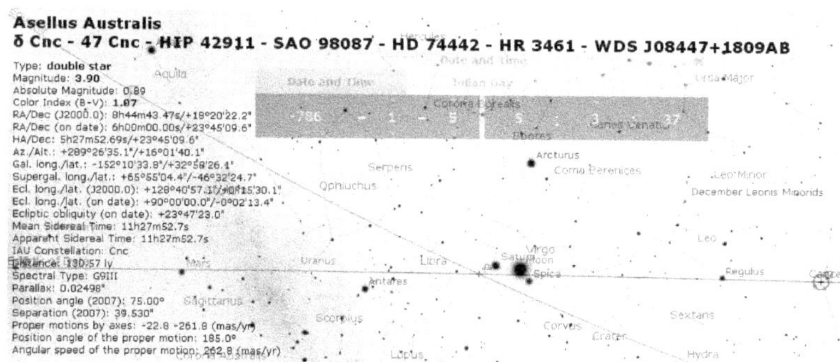

Figure 5.7: The currently accepted yogatārā of Puṣya nakṣatra on summer solstice

As described in Chapter 4, the ecliptic latitude of Arcturus (α Boo) is 30° 43′. Since the yogatārā of Swāti is far away from ecliptic, it is plausible that the ecliptic longitude of the yogatārā of Swāti falls outside the boundaries of Swāti nakṣatra. Thus, the time of Jain astronomical observations determined from the ecliptic longitude of the yogatārā of Swāti may not be accurate.

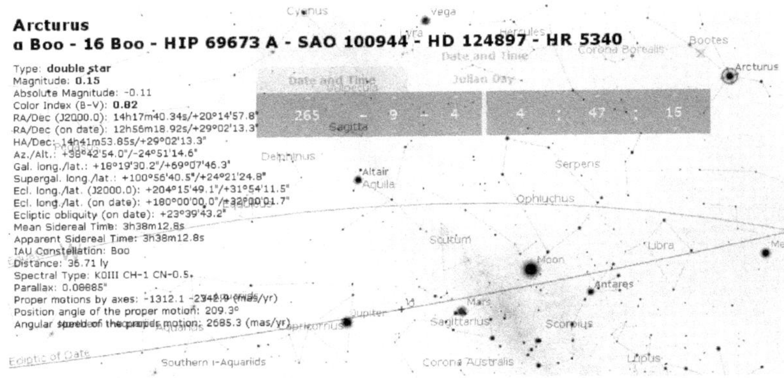

Figure 5.8: The currently accepted yogatārā of Swāti nakṣatra on autumnal equinox

A summary of the dates obtained from position of sun at solstices and equinoxes is presented in Table 5.6. We can see that the estimated dates range from 787 BCE to 901 CE based on the position of the yogatārās. Based on this method but only considering the yogatārā of Aświnī nakṣatra, Jain has calculated 579 BCE as the date of astronomical observations [6]. Jain has estimated that Sheraton (β Ari) was at vernal equinox in 446 BCE and Hamal (α Ari) was at vernal equinox in 711 BCE. An average of both values, 579 BCE, has been suggested for the date of astronomical observations given in Jain texts by Jain [6]. It is obvious that the position of the yogatārās is not reliable for estimating the date of astronomical observations as the yogatārās are only a visual aid in observing the nakṣatras. Astronomical dating can be reliable only if the boundaries of the nakṣatras are properly ascertained as the Jain astronomers have specified the nakṣatras based on the boundaries.

Table 5.6: The dating of Jain astronomical observations

Naksatra	Yogatārā	Position	Date
Puṣya	Asellus Australis (δ Cnc)	Summer solstice	787 BCE
Swāti	Arcturus (α Boo)	Autumnal equinox	265 CE
Abhijit	Vega (α Lyr)	Winter solstice	901 CE
Śravaṇa	Altair (α Aql)	Winter solstice	262 BCE
Aświnī	Sheraton (β Ari)	Vernal equinox	446 BCE
Aświnī	Hamal (α Ari)	Vernal equinox	709 BCE

We should note that the position of sun during solstices and equinoxes as shown in Figure 5.1 is consistent with the ecliptic longitudes of nakṣatras shown in Table 3.6. The ecliptic longitudes of Abhijit, Aświnī, Puṣya, and Swāti nakṣatras are 0° 0′0″ to 4° 7′52.1″, 83° 12′47.2″ to 96° 23′36.4″, 175° 28′ 31.5″ to 188° 39′ 20.7″, and 267° 44′15.7″ to 274° 19′40.3″ respectively as shown in Table 3.6. Counting from 0° 0′0″ at the beginning of Abhijit nakṣatra, 90° 0′0″ falls in Aświnī nakṣatra, 180° 0′0″ falls in Puṣya nakṣatra, and 270° 0′0″ falls in Swāti nakṣatra. Thus if winter solstice fell in Abhijit nakṣatra, then vernal equinox fell in Aświnī nakṣatra, summer solstice fell in Puṣya nakṣatra, and autumnal equinox fell in Swāti nakṣatra based on nakṣatra boundaries. The observational data shown in Tables 5.1 to 5.4 is completely consistent with the nakṣatra boundaries listed in Table 3.6. The most important task in astronomical dating is figuring out where the nakṣatra boundaries are. This can be done by fixing the origin of the Jain coordinate system on the ecliptic.

As discussed earlier, the yogatārās of Abhijit and Swāti nakṣatras are far away from ecliptic. The yogatārā of Puṣya is very faint and close to ecliptic, while the stars of Puṣya nakṣatra were more than 5° south of ecliptic according to Jain texts as shown in Table 4.3. Thus the currently accepted yogatārā of Puṣya was not among the stars belonging to Puṣya nakṣatra according to Jain astronomers. Thus the best choice for fixing the zero point of Jain nakṣatra system is the yogatārā of Aświnī nakṣatra.

The span of Aświnī nakṣatra is from 83° 12′47.2″ to 96° 23′36.4″ in Jain astronomy. Placing Hamal, the yogatārā of Aświnī nakṣatra, at 90° 0′0″ from the origin of Jain nakṣatra system will mean that Hamal is approximately 7° from the beginning of Aświnī nakṣatra in Jain nakṣatra system. In classical Hindu astronomy, the longitude of the yogatārā of Aświnī nakṣatra is 8° according to Sūrya Siddhānta 8.1-9. This will mean that the beginning of Aświnī nakṣatra in both Hindu astronomy and Jain astronomy coincided within the margin of error. The yogatārā of Aświnī nakṣatra being at the vernal equinox is consistent with all observations listed in Tables 5.1 to 5.4. The zero point of Jain coordinate system can then be considered at 90° 0′0″ from Hamal along the ecliptic towards Abhijit nakṣatra. This is of great significance for fixing the chronology of ancient Indian history as well.

5.3 Mālava era

It is the opinion of modern historians that the Vikrama era was earlier known as the Kṛta era or the Mālava era and all three have the starting date of 57 BCE [7]. There is evidence of the Kṛta and Mālava eras being equivalent. However, there is no evidence that either Kṛta era or Mālava era was equivalent to the Vikrama era. This distinction is of critical interest in the reconstruction of Indian history.

The meaning of the word Mālava in the Mālava era is itself in dispute. Some historians believe that the Mālava era was instituted by the Mālava tribe, which had a republican system of governance. The reason for this hypothesis is the use of the word *gaṇa* with Mālava, which can have two meanings. Gaṇa can mean a system of governance or a method of calculation. However, the view of Mālava era being instituted by the Mālava tribe is erroneous as the term *gaṇa* has been used to mean a method of calculation and not as a system of governance. This has been explained by Vyāsa as follows:

> Rock inscriptions found in Mandasaur made during fifth and sixth centuries call the era "Mālavānām Gaṇasthityā". However, they are made by kings ruling Mālavā such as Naravarmana, Kumāragupta, Bandhuvarmana and Prabhākara. Thus Gaṇa here does not mean a system of governance by Gaṇa, but way of counting as in Gaṇanā. [8]

Some other historians have associated the Mālava era with the tribe of Mallas, whom Greek historians have named Malloi, and described as neighbours of Oxydrakai (Kṣudraka). This theory does not hold any ground as the

Mallas and Kṣudrakas were at the northwestern boundaries of India during the invasion of Alexander in 4th century BCE, while Ujjain, the capital city of the ancient Malwa, is so old that traditionally it has been known as "Anādi Ujjayinī", the city without a beginning in time. The question then is what was the origin of the Mālava era?

The most important clue about Mālava era comes from a Sun temple in Mandsaur. This temple has two inscriptions dated in Mālava era [9]. The second inscription is a continuation of the first inscription. According to the first inscription, the Sun temple was built by a guild of silk weavers in the Mālava year 493 when Kumāragupta-I was ruling the world. The second inscription mentions that the Sun temple was repaired by the guild of silk weavers in Mālava year 529.

There are good reasons to believe that the Imperial Guptas were the contemporary of Alexander instead of the Mauryas as described in my book "India before Alexander: A New Chronology" [10]. In this alternative chronology, Chandragupta-I, the founder of the Imperial Gupta dynasty, was the contemporary of Alexander and Seleucus instead of Chandragupta Maurya. As Kumāragupta-I was the great grandson of Chandragupta-I, his date would fall towards the end of third century BCE to the beginning of second century BCE. If we match this time period with Mālava era 493 and 529 of the inscriptions, this will yield the starting date of Mālava era towards the end of eighth century BCE. Based on this argument, the dates of 725 BCE and 711 BCE have been proposed by Venkatachalam and Sethna for the starting date of Mālava era respectively.

> They arbitrarily brought Malwa Gana era from 725 B.C. to 57 B.C., and dared proclaim that this was identical with the Vikrama Era or Azes Era. [11]

> Counting from 315 B.C. as the accession-date of Chandragupta I, we get for the years 95-135 of Kumāragupta I the reign-period 220-180 B.C. … Then, to reach the starting-point of the Mālava Era, we may count either 493 years backward from 218 B.C. or 529 from 182 B.C. We arrive at 711 B.C. [12]

However, the problem with these two dates is their arbitrariness as no additional justification for the specific starting dates have been provided. The starting dates of eras usually have some historical or astronomical significance. As discussed earlier in this chapter, Hamal (α Ari), the yogatārā of Aświnī, was at the vernal equinox in 709 BCE. This is tantalizingly close to 702 BCE, when Hamal would still be seen at the vernal equinox as sun moves only 1° in 72 years due to precession of the equinoxes. In my book India after Alexander: The Age of Vikramādityas", I had proposed 702 BCE as the starting date of Mālava era based on the start of Avasarpiṇī age in 702 BCE [13]. With the discovery of the yogatārā of Aświnī at the vernal equinox being the zero point of Jain astronomy, now there is a better justification for the starting date of Mālava era in 702 BCE. The Mālava era was constituted by Jain astronomers in 702 BCE to mark the yogatārā of Aświnī at the vernal equinox. Hamal, as the brightest star of Aświnī naksatra, was an important star and it being at vernal equinox was an important event.

The discovery of the Mālava era as the zero point of Jain astronomy is an important step in the discovery of the true history of India. Indian astronomers were observing the movement of sun, moon, planets and stars since 3000 BCE. The astronomical information given in the ancient texts can be used to date these texts and understand their chronological order.

Notes

1. Triloka Prajñapti 7.533-536.
2. Triloka Prajñapti 7.541-550.
3. Triloka Prajñapti 7.537-540.
4. Sridharan (2005): 7.
5. Roy (2020).
6. Jain (1983): 31.
7. Thapar (2003): xiii.
8. Vyāsa (1990): 30.
9. Fleet (1888).
10. Roy (2015a).
11. Venkatachelam (1953).
12. Sethna (1989).
13. Roy (2015b).

"It is an unscrupulous intellect that does not pay to antiquity its due reverence."
- Desiderius Erasmus

6. Antiquity of Indian Astronomy

The performance of rituals was closely tied with the position of the sun and moon among the background of the nakṣatras. Special attention was paid to the observation of solstices and equinoxes. A story in Mahābhārata not only shows the importance of winter solstice but also the desire of the writers of Mahābhārata to carry forward this knowledge to future generations. The story is that of the death of one of the most beloved characters of Mahābhārata, Bhīṣma, and is told in Bhīṣma Parva (120.51-53). According to this story, when Bhīṣma is incapacitated on the battlefield, he refuses to die. He says that he will lie on the bed of arrows till the time of winter solstice. When sun starts its northward journey, only then he will leave this world. He waited for close to two months for winter solstice to take place and then left this world. This story has been passed on from generation to generation, and the dramatic nature of this narrative ensures that the listener will know the definition of winter solstice, which is the day when sun starts its northward journey. To make sure that the message gets passed on to future generations, a very dramatic situation was created in the storyline. From the details of the story, it is clear that the event cannot be historic as no one can control his time of death and lying on a bed of arrows for close to two months is an improbable event. What the story tells us is that winter solstice, and by implication summer solstice and equinoxes, were being carefully observed in India for many millennia. It would have been obvious to Indian astronomers that the position of sun among the stars during solstices and equinoxes was slowly changing due to the effect of precession. These positions have been recorded in Jain and Hindu texts and provide us with significant clues for the reconstruction of the history of India. Tables 6.1 and 6.2 list the position of sun among the background of nakṣatras during the solstices and equinoxes as given in various texts. It can be seen that the position of sun gradually shifted during solstices and equinoxes. These positions can be dated using modern astronomy software.

6.1. Zero point of Vedic astronomy

The list of nakṣatras given in the Vedic texts begins with Kṛttikā. However, there is evidence to suggest that the list began with Rohiṇī during an earlier period. There is a dialogue between Indra and Skanda regarding the dropping of nakṣatra Abhijit in Mahābhārata (Vana Parva, 230.8-10). In this dialogue, Indra says to Skanda that because of jealousy with Rohiṇī, her younger sister Abhijit has gone to forest to do penance.

Table 6.1: The changing position of sun during equinoxes

		Vernal equinox	Autumnal equinox
1.	Zero point of Vedic astronomy	at the beginning of Rohiṇī	at the middle of Anurādhā
2.	Kṛttikā period	In Kṛttikā	in Anurādhā and Viśākhā
3.	The period of Vedāṅga Jyotiṣa	in Bharaṇī	in Viśākhā
4.	An update of Mahābhārata	in Bharaṇī and Aświnī	in Viśākhā and Swāti
5.	Zero point of Jain astronomy	in Aświnī	in Swāti
6.	Zero point of Classical Hindu astronomy	at the beginning of Aświnī	at the middle of Citrā

Table 6.2: The changing position of sun during solstices

		Winter Solstice	Summer Solstice
1.	Zero point of Vedic astronomy	in Śatabhiṣaja	in Maghā
2.	Kṛttikā period	in Śatabhiṣaja and Dhaniṣṭhā	in Maghā and Āśleṣā
3.	The period of Vedāṅga Jyotiṣa	at the beginning of Dhaniṣṭhā	at the middle of Āśleṣā
4.	An update of Mahābhārata	in Śravaṇa	in Āśleṣā and Puṣya
5.	Zero point of Jain astronomy	in Abhijit	in Puṣya
6.	Zero point of Classical Hindu astronomy	in Uttarāṣaḍhā	in Punarvasu

Indra further says that Brahmā had fixed the counting of time from the beginning of Dhaniṣṭhā and earlier Rohiṇī was first. This story tells that during the time of this observation, it was still remembered that once upon a time Rohiṇī was the first nakṣatra. The zero point of Vedic astronomy belongs to a period when the yogatārā of Rohiṇī was at vernal equinox. As shown in Figure 6.1, the yogatārā of Rohiṇī, Aldebaran, was at vernal equinox in 3045 BCE. Thus the origin of Indian astronomy can be traced to ~3,000 BCE. At this time, sun was at the boundary of Rohiṇī and Kṛttikā nakṣatras during vernal equinox, in Maghā nakṣatra during summer solstice, at the middle of Anurādhā nakṣatra during autumnal equinox, and in Śatabhiṣaja nakṣatra during winter solstice.

6.2. Kṛttikā period

Vedic text Taittirīya Saṃhitā (iv.4.10) starts the list of nakṣatra with Kṛttikā signifying sun being in Kṛttikā nakṣatra during vernal equinox. As shown in Figure 6.2, the yogatārā of Kṛttikā, Alcyone, was at vernal equinox in 2337 BCE. Thus the Kṛttikā period falls in third millennium BCE and is contemporaneous with Indus Valley Civilization. During this period, sun was in Kṛttikā nakṣatra during vernal equinox, in Maghā and Āśleṣā nakṣatras during summer solstice, in Anurādhā and Viśākhā nakṣatras during autumnal equinox, and in Śatabhiṣaja and Dhaniṣṭhā nakṣatras during winter solstice. An explicit statement of this observation is found in the Maitrāyaṇa Brāhmaṇa Upaniṣad (6.14) which says that summer solstice was at the junction of Maghā and Āśleṣā while the winter solstice was in the middle of Śravishṭhā (Dhanishṭhā).

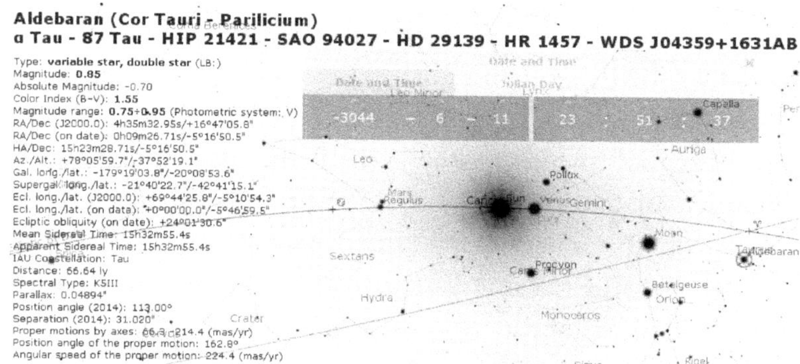

Figure 6.1: Zero point of Vedic astronomy (the yogatārā of Rohiṇī, Aldebaran, at vernal equinox in ~3,000 BCE)

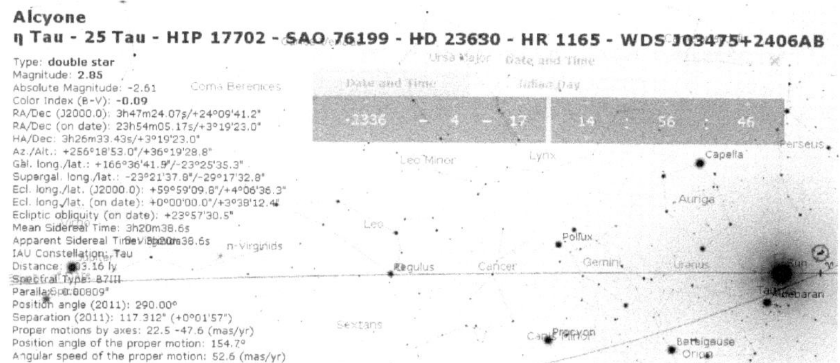

Figure 6.2: Kṛttikā period (the yogatārā of Kṛttikā, Alcyone, at vernal equinox in ~2,300 BCE)

6.3. The period of Vedāṅga Jyotiṣa

The Vedāṅga Jyotiśa is the first astronomical text of ancient India. It is mentioned in the verses 6-8 of the Yajuṣ Vedāṅga Jyotiṣa that the winter solstice was at the beginning of the Śraviṣṭhā (Dhaniṣṭhā) nakṣatra and the summer solstice was at the midpoint of the Āśleṣā nakṣatra. Based on this observation, the Vedāṅga Jyotiśa is dated between 1150 BCE to 1400 BCE [1]. However, this date is based on the identification of Rotanev (β Delphini) as the yogatārā of Dhaniṣṭhā nakṣatra and it being 3° inside the Dhaniṣṭhā nakṣatra. The position of the yogatārā of Dhaniṣṭhā nakṣatra is 3° 20′ outside Dhaniṣṭhā nakṣatra according to Sūrya Siddhānta (8.1-9). Based on a detailed analysis, author has proposed that the yogatārā of Dhaniṣṭhā nakṣatra should be identified with Al Salib (γ2 Delphini) [2]. As shown in Figure 6.3, Al Salib was 3° 20′ from vernal equinox in 1831 BCE. Accordingly, the date of composition of the Vedāṅga Jyotiśa was ~1850 BCE.

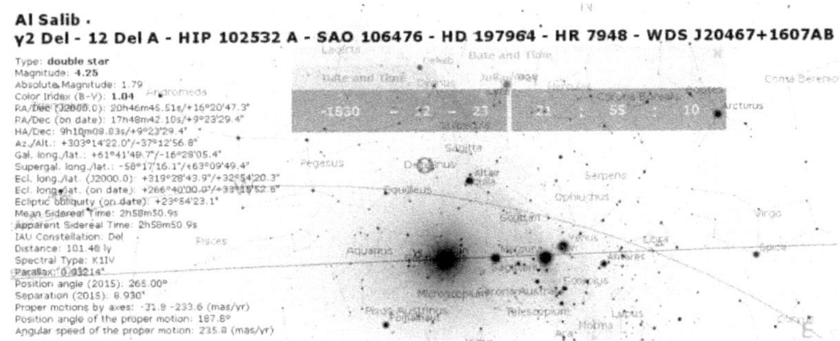

Figure 6.3: The period of Vedāṅga Jyotiṣa (the yogatārā of Dhaniṣṭhā, Al Salib, at 3°20′ from winter solstice in ~1,850 BCE)

Thus the Vedāṅga Jyotiśa was composed soon after the end of mature phase of Indus Valley Civilization. At this time, sun was in Bharaṇī and Aświnī nakṣatras during vernal equinox, at the middle of Āśleṣā nakṣatra during summer solstice, in Viśākhā nakṣatra during autumnal equinox, and at the beginning of Dhaniṣṭhā nakṣatra during winter solstice.

6.4. An update of Mahābhārata

According to two observations in Mahābhārata, sun was in Bharaṇī and Aświnī nakṣatras during vernal equinox, in Āśleṣā and Puṣya nakṣatras during summer solstice, in Viśākhā and Swāti nakṣatras during autumnal equinox, and in Śravaṇa nakṣatra during winter solstice. A story in Mahābhārata refers to this period in a dramatic way. It is told that Viśwāmitra created a new world in which the first nakshatra was Śravaṇa [3]. Elsewhere in Mahābhārata also it is stated that nakṣatras started from Śravaṇa [4]. These references refer to the sun being in Śravaṇa nakṣatra during winter solstice. The time period of this observation is second millennium BCE. Around the middle of this period, the yogatārā of Bharaṇī was at vernal equinox. As shown in Figure 6.4, the yogatārā of Bharaṇī, Bharani, was at vernal equinox in ~1,500 BCE.

6.5. Zero point of Jain astronomy

The zero point of Jain astronomy has been discussed in detail in the previous chapter. Hamal, the yogatārā of Aświnī, was at the vernal equinox during this time. As shown in Figure 6.5, the time period of Jain astronomy is ~700 BCE.

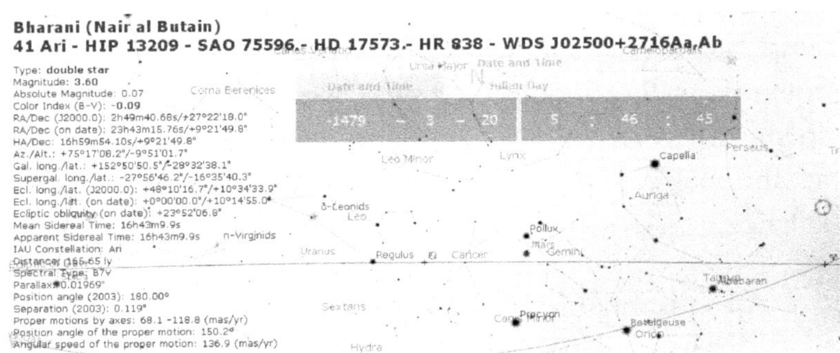

Figure 6.4: An update of Mahābhārata (the yogatārā of Bharaṇī, Bharani, at vernal equinox in ~1,500 BCE)

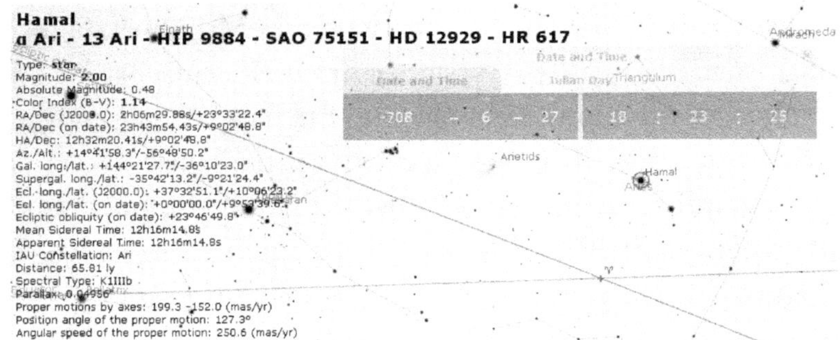

Figure 6.5: Zero point of Jain astronomy (the yogatārā of Aświnī, Hamal, at vernal equinox in ~700 BCE)

During this time, sun was in Aświnī nakṣatra during vernal equinox, in Puṣya nakṣatra during summer solstice, in Swāti nakṣatra during autumnal equinox, and in Abhijit nakṣatra during winter solstice.

6.6. Zero point of Classical Hindu astronomy

During this time, sun was at the beginning of Aświnī nakṣatra during vernal equinox, in Punarvasu nakṣatra during summer solstice, at the midpoint of Citrā nakṣatra during autumnal equinox, and in Uttarāṣaḍhā nakṣatra during winter solstice. A statement to this effect has been made by celebrated astronomer Varāhamihira [5]. He has made the observation that during his time, sun turned southward from the beginning of Karkaṭaka and turned northward from the beginning of Makara. This is equivalent to the positions of sun during solstices and equinoxes as described above. A detailed analysis is given in author's book "Zero points of Vedic Astronomy" [2]. At this time, Hamal, the yogatārā of Aświnī, had an ecliptic longitude of 8^0, since Hamal is located at 8^0 from the beginning of Aświnī naksatra according to Sūrya Siddhānta (8.1-9). As shown in Figure 6.6, the date of this event was ~150 BCE.

As described above, the position of sun changed gradually from the beginning of Rohiṇī to the beginning of Aświnī during vernal equinox, from Maghā to Punarvasu during summer solstice, from the middle of Anurādhā to the middle of Citrā during autumnal equinox, and from Śatabhiṣaja to Uttarāṣaḍhā during winter solstice. These positions are shown illustratively in Figures 6.7 and 6.8.

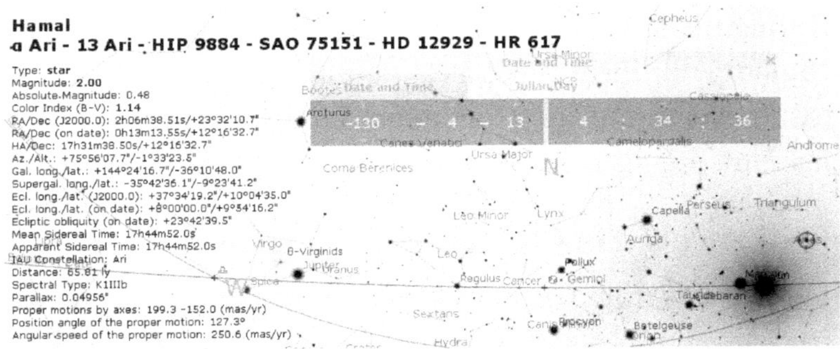

Figure 6.6: Zero point of Classical Hindu astronomy (the yogatārā of Aświnī, Hamal, at 8° from vernal equinox in ~150 BCE)

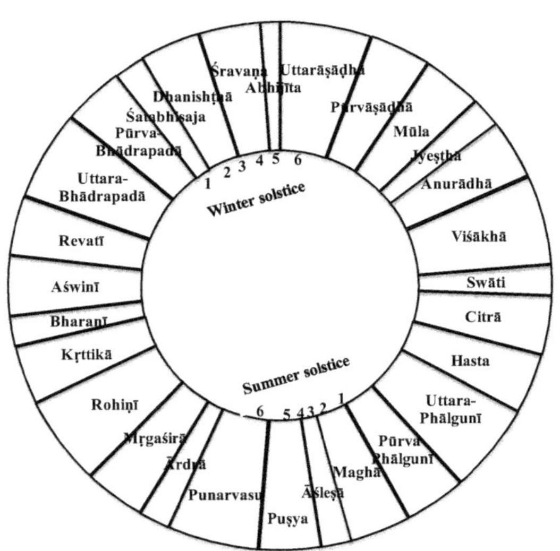

Figure 6.7: The changing position of sun during solstices 1. Zero point of Vedic astronomy; 2. Kṛttikā period; 3. The period of Vedāṅga Jyotiṣa; 4. An update of Mahābhārata; 5. Zero point of Jain astronomy; and 6. Zero point of Classical Hindu astronomy

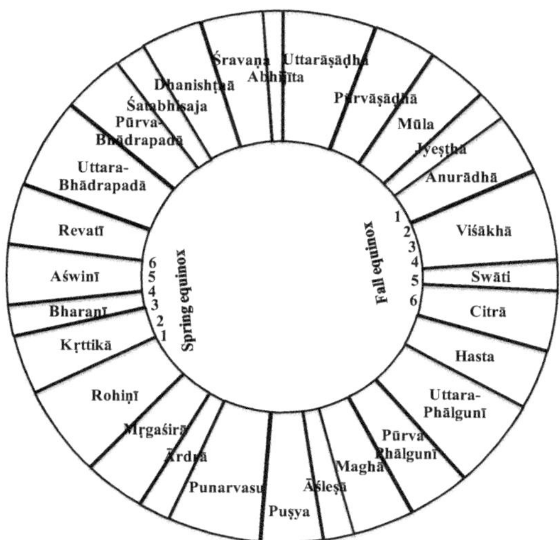

Figure 6.8: The changing position of sun during equinoxes 1. Zero point of Vedic astronomy; 2. Kṛttikā period; 3. The period of Vedāṅga Jyotiṣa; 4. An update of Mahābhārata; 5. Zero point of Jain astronomy; and 6. Zero point of Classical Hindu astronomy

The careful observation of the motions of sun, moon, and stars led to the making of Vedic calendar, which forms the basis of Jain calendar as described in Jain texts.

Notes

1. Kuppanna Sastry (1985): 13-15.
2. Roy (2020).
3. Mahābhārata, Ādi Parva, Chapter 71, verse 34.
4. Mahābhārata, Aśvamedha Parva, Chapter 44, Verse 2.
5. Bṛhat Saṃhitā 3.2.

"The only reason for time is so that everything doesn't happen at once."
- Albert Einstein

7. The Jain Calendar

Before the mechanical watches were invented, it was common all over the world to measure time from the shadow of a gnomon or water clock. Water clocks measured time from the rate of flow of water from a water vessel with a hole in the bottom. In India, sundials on the walls of Koṇārka temple show time to the accuracy of a minute. Estimation of time and season from the length of shadows is described in detail in Jain astronomical texts. The measurement of time from water clock is described in Vedāṅga Jyotiṣa.

7.1. Measurement of time

According to Vedāṅga Jyotiṣa, a volume of 61 kudava of water flows from the standard water vessel in 1 nāḍikā [1]. To get a feel for this in the units we are familiar with, we need to know the ancient Indian units of volume and time as shown in Tables 7.1 and 7.2.

Table 7.1: Volume measures in ancient India [2]

Unit	Conversion	Modern equivalent
1 kudava		74.0 cc
1 prastha	4 kudava	295.9 cc
1 āḍhaka	4 prastha	1.2 litre
1 droṇa	4 ādhaka	4.7 litre
1 khāri	16 droṇa	75.8 litre
1 kumbha	20 droṇa	94.7 litre
1 vāha	10 kumbha	946.9 litre

Table 7.2: Time measures in ancient India [3]

Unit	Conversion	Modern equivalent
1 akṣara		231.1 milliseconds
1 kāṣṭha	5 akṣara	1.16 seconds
1 pāda	31 kāṣṭhas	35.82 seconds
1 kalā	4 pāda	2.39 minutes
1 nāḍikā	10 and 1/20 kalā	24 minutes
1 muhūrta	2 nāḍikā	48 minutes
1 ahna	30 muhūrta	1 day
1 ayana	183 ahna	6 months
1 abda	2 ayana	1 year
1 yuga	5 abda	5 years

In Table 7.1, the conversion of volume from ancient Indian units to modern units has been done based on information from Bhaskar. In Līlāvatī, Bhaskar says that khāri equals a cube of a hasta, which he describes as 24 aṅgula long [4]. Aṅgula has a standard length of 1.763 cm starting from Indus Valley Civilization [5, 6]. Based on this information, volume of khāri can be calculated and the volume of other units can be calculated from the volume of khāri as shown in Table 7.1. As 61 kudava of water flows in 1 nāḍikā according to Vedāṅga Jyotiṣa, this is equivalent to a flow of 4.5 litre of water in 24 minutes from the standard water vessel based on Tables 7.1 and 7.2. We should note that there were variations in the conversion factors for different units over time and among different regions.

Estimation of time from the length of shadow is described in Jain astronomical treatise Sūrya Prajñapti. Following information is given in Sūrya Prajñapti 9:

> Sun produces a shadow of 59 pauruṣī length at the beginning of the day. When the shadow is of 1/2 pauruṣī length, then 1/3 of the day has already elapsed. When the shadow is of 1 pauruṣī length, then 1/4 of the day has already elapsed. When the shadow is of 1 and 1/2 pauruṣī length, then 1/5 of the day has already elapsed. Relationship between shadow length and fraction of day elapsed continues in this manner.

This information is shown graphically in Figure 7.1. A detailed analysis shows that this information matches very well with actual data given by modern astronomy [7]. The information given in Sūrya Prajñapti is compared with the data from Ujjain and Taxila in Figure 7.2.

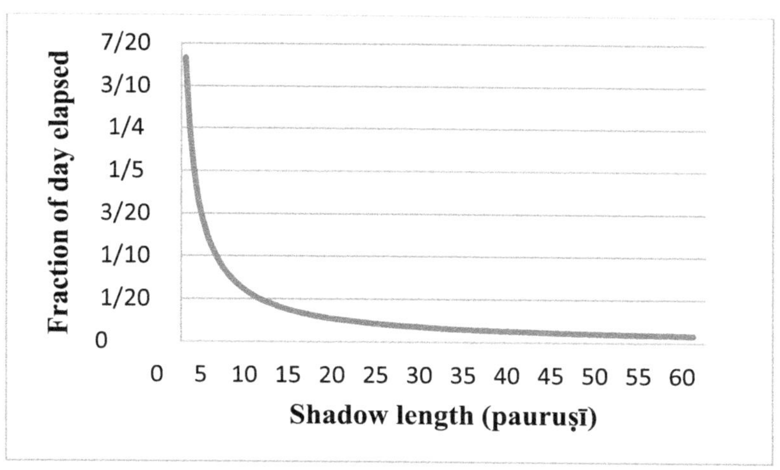

Figure 7.1: Relation of shadow length with fraction of day elapsed according to Sūrya Prajñapti 9

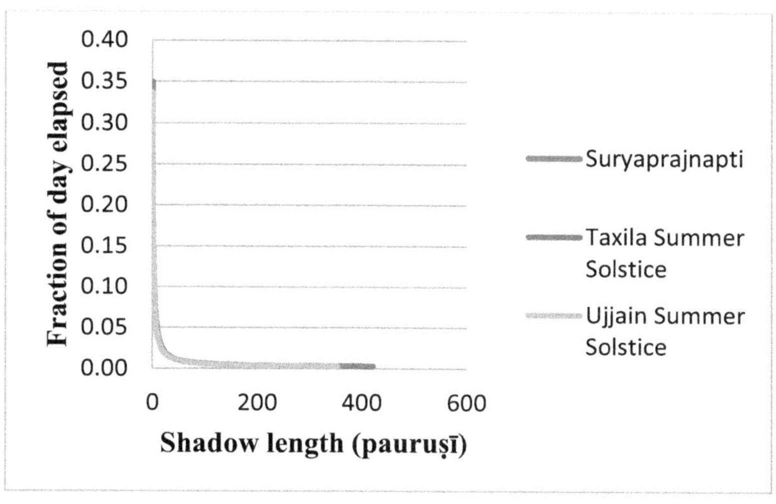

Figure 7.2: Comparison of the variation of shadow length with fraction of day elapsed on summer solstice

Ujjain (latitude 23.18°) and Taxila (latitude 33.74°) cover the extreme latitudes of North India, where the information given in Jain texts was generated. The data from modern astronomy matches the data given in Sūrya Prajñapti 9 so well that the different curves are nearly indistinguishable due to data being so close to each other. Though the data best fits the actual data from Ujjain on summer solstice, it is applicable to whole of north India over the duration of whole year to a reasonable degree. This shows that ancient Jain astronomers made very careful observation of the variation of shadow length with time of the day and derived a mathematical relationship that was applicable over a large region during the course of whole year.

7.2. Seasons

Jain texts divide the year in three seasons of four months each. Table 7.3 shows the seasons and months of the Jain calendar. Jain and Hindu texts provide information on the variation of shadow length with seasons. Following information is given in Jain text Sūrya Prajñapti 10.10 regarding the length of shadows formed at the end of each month (at noon).

> At the end of Śrāvaṇa, first month of rainy season, the length of Pauruṣī shadow is 2 pāda and 4 aṅgula. At the end of Bhādrapada, second month of rainy season, the length of Pauruṣī shadow is 2 pāda and 8 aṅgula. At the end of Āśvina, third month of rainy season, the length of Pauruṣī shadow is 3 pāda. At the end of Kārttika, fourth month of rainy season, the length of Pauruṣī shadow is 3 pāda and 4 aṅgula. At the end of Mārgaśīrṣa, first month of winter season, the length of Pauruṣī shadow is 3 pāda and 8 aṅgula. At the end of Pauṣa, second month of

winter season, the length of Paurușī shadow is 4 pāda. At the end of Māgha, third month of winter season, the length of Paurușī shadow is 3 pāda and 8 aṅgula. At the end of Phālguna, fourth month of winter season, the length of Paurușī shadow is 3 pāda and 4 aṅgula. At the end of Caitra, first month of summer season, the length of Paurușī shadow is 3 pāda. At the end of Vaiśākha, second month of summer season, the length of Paurușī shadow is 2 pāda and 8 aṅgula. At the end of Jyeṣṭha, third month of summer season, the length of Paurușī shadow is 2 pāda and 4 aṅgula. At the end of Āṣāḍha, fourth month of summer season, the length of Paurușī shadow is 2 pāda.

Table 7.3: Months and seasons in Jain calendar

Season	Month
Varṣā (Rainy)	1. Śrāvaṇa
	2. Bhādrapada
	3. Āśvina
	4. Kārttika
Hemanta (Winter)	1. Mārgaśīrṣa
	2. Pauṣa
	3. Māgha
	4. Phālguna
Grīṣma (Summer)	1. Caitra
	2. Vaiśākha
	3. Jyeṣṭha
	4. Āṣāḍha

It is obvious from the information given in Sūrya Prajñapti 10.10 that one pāda is considered equal to 12 aṅgula. Based on this conversion, the total length of shadow at the end of each month is shown in Table 7.4 and Figure 7.3. The length of shadow is shortest at the end of summer and equals 24 aṅgula. It increases by 4 aṅgula every month till it is longest six months later in the middle of winter and equals 48 aṅgula. It then decreases by 4 aṅgula every month till it is shortest again at the end of next summer and equals 24 aṅgula.

Table 7.4: Length of shadow during the year according to Sūrya Prajñapti 10.10

Month	Name of month	Pauruṣī shadow		
		pāda	aṅgula	Total (aṅgula)
1	Śrāvaṇa	2	4	28
2	Bhādrapada	2	8	32
3	Āśvina	3	0	36
4	Kārttika	3	4	40
5	Mārgaśīrṣa	3	8	44
6	Pauṣa	4	0	48
7	Māgha	3	8	44
8	Phālguna	3	4	40
9	Caitra	3	0	36
10	Vaiśakha	2	8	32
11	Jyeṣṭha	2	4	28
12	Āṣāḍha	2	0	24

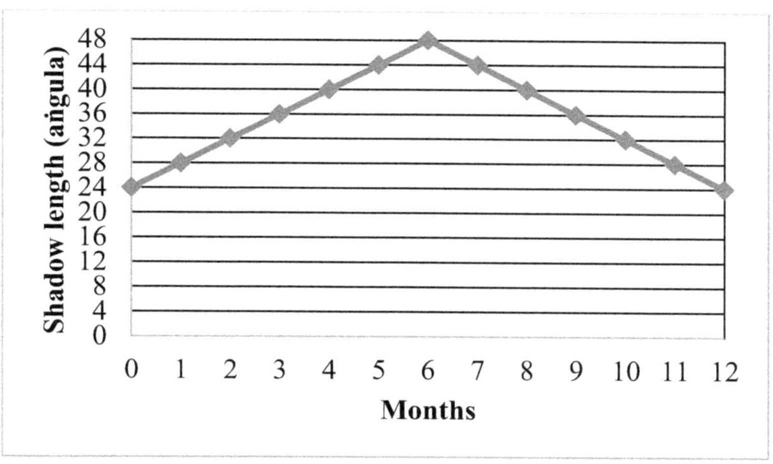

Figure 7.3: Length of shadow during the year according to Sūrya Prajñapti 10.10

As shown in Table 7.4 and Figure 7.3, shadow length increases in a linear manner from the end of summer (summer solstice) to middle of winter (winter solstice) and then decreases in a linear manner from the middle of winter (winter solstice) to summer (summer solstice) according to Sūrya Prajñapti 10.10.

The information presented in Sūrya Prajñapti 10.10 does not match any location in India. Lishk has proposed that this information was obtained in Sri Lanka [8]. After a detailed analysis, author has shown that a location in Sri Lanka is incompatible with astronomical data presented in Sūrya Prajñapti [9]. It makes no sense historically and pragmatically as well. From historical perspective, during the time of writing of Sūrya Prajñapti, Jainism was confined to north India. From a pragmatic point of view, why would astronomers be sent to a faraway place in Sri

Lanka for making such a simple measurement as to measuring the length of a shadow?

There is similar information on the length of shadows formed at the end of each month (at noon) in Kauṭilya's Arthaśāstra 2.20.41 as follows. In the month of Āṣāḍha, there is no shadow at midday. After that, in the six months beginning with Śrāvaṇa, the shadow increases by two aṅgula every month. The shadow decreases by two aṅgula every month beginning with Māgha. This information is shown graphically in Figure 7.4. The minimum shadow length for a gnomon of 12 aṅgula height on 21st day of each month at Ujjain is also added for comparison. This data was obtained using an astronomy software [10]. A gnomon of 12 aṅgula height was typically used in India [11]. Since Arthaśāstra 2.20.41 mentions that there was no shadow at midday on summer solstice, it is clear that the point of observation was close to the Tropic of Cancer, and hence Ujjain. It can be seen that the data in Arthaśāstra matches well with data obtained using modern astronomy. The data in Arthaśāstra 2.20.41 can be considered to be a linearized version of actual observation. The question is if the data in Arthaśāstra 2.20.41 is so close to modern astronomical data, then why there is no match for the data in Sūrya Prajñapti 10.10?

A comparison of data from Sūrya Prajñapti and Arthaśāstra shows that the shadow length given in Sūrya Prajñapti is generated by a gnomon that is twice the length compared to that used in Arthaśāstra and it has an offset of 24 aṅgula. Since the gnomon height is 12 aṅgula for the information given in Arthaśāstra, the gnomon height is 24 aṅgula for the information given in Sūrya Prajñapti. An offset of 24 aṅgula can be generated by a wedge-shaped gnomon instead of a rod-shaped gnomon. Such a gnomon will make shadows that will match closely with the information given in Sūrya Prajñapti 10.10 [9].

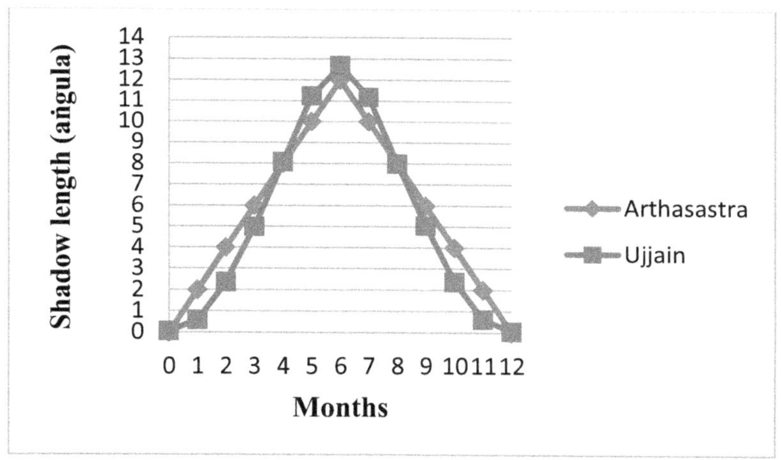

Figure 7.4: Comparison of minimum shadow length at Ujjain with Arthaśāstra

Figure 7.5 compares the shadow generated by the wedge-shaped gnomon at Ujjain with the information given in Sūrya Prajñapti 10.10. It can be seen that the shadow lengths given in Sūrya Prajñapti match very well with the shadow lengths generated using a wedge-shaped gnomon.

Based on the information presented, it can be said that Jain astronomers made very careful observations, which need to be properly understood in the light of modern astronomy.

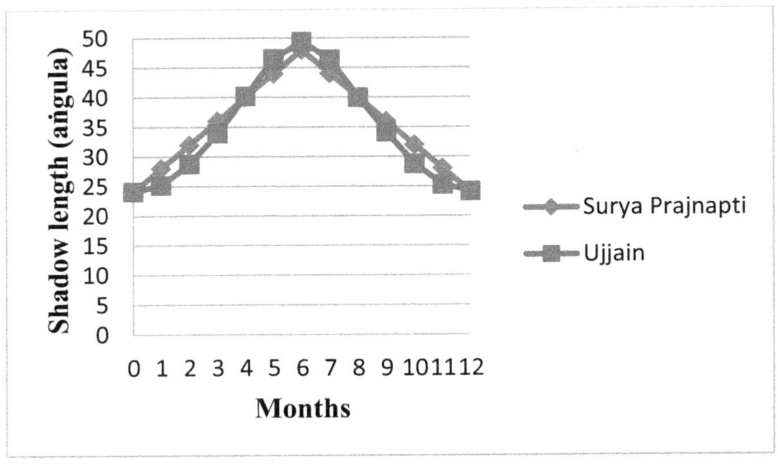

Figure 7.5: Comparison of minimum shadow length of wedge shaped gnomon at Ujjain with Sūrya Prajñapti

7.3. Different types of years

According to Sūrya Prajñapti 12.72, there are five types of years (samvatsara). They are called Nakṣatra samvatsara, Candra samvatsara, Ṛtu samvatsara, Āditya samvatsara, and Abhivarddhita samvatsara.

7.3.1: Nakṣatra samvatsara

Nakṣatra samvatsara is based on the concept of sidereal month, which is the time taken by the moon to complete one full revolution around the Earth. From earth, this looks like a complete revolution of moon in the background of the stars. A lunar sidereal month is 27.322 days long. A lunar sidereal year equals 12 lunar sidereal months and is 327.864 days long.

A Nakṣatra samvatsara equals 12 lunar sidereal months. According to Sūrya Prajñapti 12.72, there are 27 and 21/67 days or 819 and 27/67 muhūrtas in a Nakṣatra month. Both of these values are equal, as there are 30 muhūrtas in a day of 24 hours. Thus a Nakṣatra month is 27.313 days long. There were 327 and 51/67 days or 9832 and 56/67 muhūrtas in a Nakṣatra samvatsara. Thus a Nakṣatra samvatsara is 327.761 days long. The values of Nakṣatra month and Nakṣatra samvatsara compare well with modern values.

7.3.2: Candra samvatsara

Candra samvatsara is based on the concept of synodic month, which is the time between a new moon and next new moon. Lunar synodic month is longer than lunar sidereal month because of earth's rotation around the sun. The moon needs to travel further to align with the earth and sun as the earth has moved further. The duration of a lunar sidereal month is 27.322 days, while the duration of a lunar synodic month is 29.531 days. A lunar synodic year equals 12 lunar synodic months and is 354.372 days long.

A Candra samvatsara equals 12 lunar synodic months. According to Sūrya Prajñapti 12.72, there are 29 and 32/62 days or 885 and 30/60 muhūrtas in a Candra month. Thus a Candra month is 29.516 days long. There were 354 and 12/62 days or 10,625 and 50/62 muhūrtas in a Candra samvatsara. Thus a Candra samvatsara is 354.194 days long. The values of Candra month and Candra samvatsara compare well with modern values.

7.3.3: Ṛtu samvatsara

Ṛtu samvatsara or seasonal year is 360 days or 10,800 muhūrtas long and is based on a seasonal (Ṛtu) month of 30 days or 900 muhūrtas.

7.3.4: Āditya samvatsara

Āditya samvatsara or solar year is 366 days or 10,980 muhūrtas long and is based on a solar (Āditya) month of 30.5 days or 915 muhūrtas.

7.3.5: Abhivarddhita samvatsara

Abhivarddhita samvatsara or extended year is 383 days and 21 and 18/62 muhūrtas long or equivalently 11,511 and 18/62 muhūrtas long and is based on an extended (Abhivarddhita) month of 31 days and 29 and 17/62 muhūrtas or equivalently 959 and 17/62 muhūrtas. Thus the Abhivarddhita month is 31.976 days long and the Abhivarddhita samvatsara is 383.710 days long. The concept of Abhivarddhita samvatsara is related to the 5-year Yuga.

7.4. The concept of Yuga

The word yuga comes from the root "yuja", which means to join. The concept of 5-year yuga was developed based on the joining of the various periods of sun and moon described above. A 5-year yuga consists of 5 solar years (Āditya samvatsara) and is thus 1,830 days long. As shown in Table 7.5, a yuga of 1,830 days results in integral number of Nakṣatra, Candra, Ṛtu, and Āditya months in a yuga.

Table 7.5: The concept of 5-year yuga

Type of year	Duration of year	Duration of month	Number of months	Number of days
Nakṣatra samvatsara	327.761 days	27 and 21/67 days	67	1,830
Candra samvatsara	354.194 days	29 and 32/62 days	62	1,830
Ṛtu samvatsara	360 days	30 days	61	1,830
Āditya samvatsara	366 days	30 and 1/2 days	60	1,830
Abhivarddhita samvatsara	383.710	31 days and 29 and 17/62 muhūrtas		

In a 5 year yuga, number of lunar synodic months is 62, while the number of solar months is 60. This means that two lunar synodic months need to be added over a 5 year period to synchronize lunar and solar calendars. This is done by adding an extra lunar synodic month during third and fifth year. The year with additional lunar months is called Abhivarddhita samvatsara. Its duration is exactly 13 lunar synodic months. The duration of the Abhivarddhita month is obtained by dividing the duration of Abhivarddhita samvatsara by twelve. According to Sūrya Prajñapti 10.20.3, the order of samvatsara is Candra, Candra, Abhivarddhita, Candra, and Abhivarddhita in a yuga.

7.5. The Pañcāṅga

The calendar is called pañcāṅga, which is made by joining words pañca (five) and aṅga (limbs). The five limbs of pañcāṅga are vāra, tithi, nakṣatra, yoga, and karaṇa.

Vāra: Vāra is the name of the seven days in a week, Somavāra (Monday), Maṅgalavāra (Tuesday), Budhavāra (Wednesday), Guruvāra (Thursday), Śukravāra (Friday), Śanivāra (Saturday), and Raviavāra (Sunday).

Tithi: Tithi is the equivalent of date in western calendar, but is based on the phase of the moon. The synodic or lunar month is approximately 29.5 days long, which is divided in 30 tithis. Mathematically, one tithi is the time taken by the moon in increasing its distance from the sun by 12 degrees, making a complete circle of 360^0 in 30 tithis. At the moment of amāvasyā (new moon), the difference in their longitudes is 0° as the sun and moon are in same direction from earth at that time. At the moment of Pūrṇimā (full moon), the difference in their longitudes is 180° as the sun and moon are at opposite sides of earth at that time. The length of tithi varies between 22 hours and 26 hours as the angular velocity of moon's movement is not constant. Each lunar month is divided in two pakṣas (fortnights), śukla pakṣa (bright fortnight) and kṛṣṇa pakṣa (dark fortnight). The Tithis are specified by specifying the pakṣa and ordinal number within the pakṣa.

Nakṣatra: The concept of nakṣatra has been described in detail in Chapter 3. Nakṣatra is specified by the name of the nakṣatra in which moon resides at that point in time.

Yoga: Yoga is the length of time during which the distance between the sun and the moon is increased by 13° 20′. As this distance varies from 0° to 360° in a lunar month, there are 27 yogas in a lunar month.

Karaṇa: Karaṇa is half of the tithi. Mathematically, one karaṇa is the time taken by the moon in increasing its distance from the sun by 6 degrees.

With a clear understanding of the timekeeping in ancient India, we will now focus on whether the timeline of Indian history needs a revision.

Notes

1. Yajus Vedāṅga Jyotiṣa 24.
2. Arthaśāstra 2.32-50.
3. Kuppanna Sastry (1985): 38-39.
4. Srinivasan (1979): 74.
5. Danino (2005).
6. Danino (2008).
7. Roy (2018a).
8. Lishk (1987): 98-109.
9. Roy (2018b).
10. https://www.suncalc.org/.
11. Ohashi (1994).

"The right understanding of any matter and a misunderstanding of the same matter do not wholly exclude each other."

— Franz Kafka

8. The Dating of Lord Mahāvīra

According to well established Jain traditions given in Paṭṭāvalīs, the Nirvāṇa of Lord Mahāvīra took place 470 years before Vikram era. Jain texts provide breakdown of the intervening period as shown in Table 8.1 [1]:

Table 8.1: Kings after the Nirvāṇa of Lord Mahāvīra

King	Reign period
Pālaka	60 years
The Nandas	155 years
The Mauryas	108 years
Puṣyamitra	30 years
Balamitra-Bhānumitra	60 years
Naravāhana	40 years
Gardabhilla	13 years
Śaka	4 years
Total	470 years

Counting from 57 BCE, this gives 527 BCE as the year of Nirvāṇa of Lord Mahāvīra. Since Lord Mahāvīra lived for 72 years, he lived between 599 BCE to 527 BCE according to Jain traditions. This creates a problem for modern historians as they have placed the birth of Lord Buddha sometime between 567-563 BCE and his Nirvāṇa sometime between 487-483 BCE. The Nirvāṇa of Lord Mahāvīra more than 40 years before Lord Buddha would make him too much senior than Lord Buddha, so they had to bring the date of Lord Mahāvīra closer to the date of Lord Buddha. Jacobi had achieved that by proposing that the period between the Nirvāṇa of Lord Mahāvīra and Vikram era should not include the 60 years of Pālaka:

> Pālaka had, most probably, no place in the original chronology of the Jains. He is, I am inclined to believe, a mere chronological fiction of the Jains introduced in order to make it better agree with the Buddhist chronology of Ceylon. [2]

The argument is really strange, because it is the modern historians who have put so much faith in the Buddhist chronology of Ceylon and derived the date of Lord Buddha from Ceylonese chronicles. Why would Jains of India have bothered about the belief of the Buddhists in Ceylon? Based on this spurious argument of neglecting the rule of Pālaka, the coronation of Chandragupta Maurya is taken 155 years after the Nirvāṇa of Lord Mahāvīra. The coronation of Chandragupta Maurya took place 255 years before Vikrama era according to the list above, or in 312 BCE. The Nirvāṇa of Lord Mahāvīra is thus placed in 467 BCE and his birth 72 years earlier in 539 BCE. The whole argument totally neglects the other piece of information in Jain texts according to which Lord Mahāvīra's Nirvāṇa coincided with the coronation of Pālaka, who had ruled for sixty years. Another variation of this force-fitting of evidence has been given by Seth, who has argued that Lord

Mahāvīra's Nirvāṇa took place in 488 BCE [3]. To arrive at this date, he simply neglects the rule of Naravāhana, thus deducting 40 years from the 470 year interval between the Nirvāṇa of Lord Mahāvīra and Vikram era. Counting from 58 BCE as the beginning of Vikram era instead of 57 BCE and assuming 430 years between the Nirvāṇa of Lord Mahāvīra and Vikram era instead of 470 years, he arrives at 488 BCE as the year of the Nirvāṇa of Lord Mahāvīra. The aim is to show that the Nirvāṇa of Lord Mahāvīra took place before the Nirvāṇa of Lord Buddha as implied by some Buddhist texts. The evidence to this effect is not very solid though as pointed out by Basham:

> We suggest that the Pāli record may not in fact refer to the death of Mahāvīra at Pāvā, but to that of Gosāla at Sāvatthi, which the Bhagavatī Sūtra also mentions as having been accompanied by quarrelling and confusion. At a later date, when the chief rival of Buddhism was no longer Ājīvikism but Jainism, the name may have been altered to add to the significance of the account. [4]

Having shown that the current dating of Lord Mahāvīra by modern historians is arbitrary, let's try to derive a new date of Lord Mahāvīra based on Jain traditions. Our most important clue is that Jain traditions held that the Nirvāṇa of Lord Mahāvīra took place 470 years before Vikram era. It is my proposition that over the course of more than two millennia Jains have substituted Mālava era with Vikram era as they are both related to the history and legends of Vikramāditya. According to modern historians, both Mālava era and Vikram era are identical. In fact, the history books teach us that there is another era, Kṛta era that is identical to both Mālava era and Vikram era. The question is how do they know that? There is an inscription of Aulikara king Naravarman written in year 461 in which Mālava era has been called Kṛta era [5], but there is no inscription that equates either Mālava era or Kṛta era with Vikram era.

The zero point of Mālava Era has to have some relation to the region known as Malwa. The most obvious connection is to the story of Vikramāditya, who was the emperor of Malwa region according to Hindu-Jain traditions. Vikramāditya ruled from the city of Ujjayinī, the capital of Malwa region.

As discussed in Chapter 2, the reversal in the path of sun at Ujjayinī formed the basis of the legend of Vikramāditya. Due to its location at the Tropic of Cancer Ujjayinī became the most prominent centre for astronomical research in ancient India and the prime meridian of the ancient world in the manner of Greenwich today. This intimate connection between Vikramāditya and Malwa region became the reason for the confusion between Mālava era and Vikrama era.

As both the Mālava era and the Vikrama era have Jain origins, Jain authors later got confused between these eras. They had the memory of the era starting 470 years after the Nirvāṇa of Lord Mahāvīra. It was shown in Chapter 5 that the zero point of Mālava Era was in 702 BCE. If we count 470 years from the beginning of Mālava era in 702 BCE, the Nirvāṇa of Lord Mahāvīra took place in 1172 BCE. As Lord Mahāvīra had lived for 72 years, he lived between 1244-1172 BCE. This new date needs to be consistent with the evidence that Lord Buddha and Lord Mahāvīra were contemporaries. We will take the dating of Lord Buddha next.

Notes:

1. Pandeya (1951): 26.
2. Eggermont (1968): 69.
3. Jain (1991): 77-78.
4. Basham (1951): 75.
5. Shastri (1996): 35-65.

"It is better to understand little than to misunderstand a lot."
—Anatole France

9. The Dating of Lord Buddha

Due to the central position of Lord Buddha in ancient Indian history, it is of paramount importance to correctly fix his date. Lord Buddha is the most dynamic and mesmerizing personality from ancient India. A number of dates for Lord Buddha have been proposed depending on the source of information. A good summary of these proposed dates was presented in a conference paper by Siglinde Dietz titled "The Dating of the Historical Buddha in the History of Western Scholarship up to 1980" [1]. The earliest dating of the Lord Buddha known to Europeans was presented in the work Confucius Sinarum Philosophus sive scietia Sinesis Latine exposita in 1687. This book was compiled by 17 Jesuits and gave the year 1026 BCE as the birth of the Lord Buddha and dated his Nirvāṇa to 947/46 BCE. In 1738 Capuchin monk Father Francesco Orazio della Penna gave 959 BCE as the year of Lord Buddha's birth. In 1756 Joseph Deguignes wrote in "Histoire generale des Huns, des Turcs, des Mongols, et des autres Tartares occidentaux" that according to the majority of historians, Lord Buddha was born in Kashmir around the year 1027 BCE. In 1788 Sir William Jones weighed the various sources and accepted 1027 BCE as the date of the Lord Buddha's birth. In 1799 Francis Buchanan presented a number of dates for Lord Buddha's life, 1028 BCE according to Chinese, 544 BCE according to Siamese and 542 BCE according to Singhalese. In 1805 J.H. Harrington considered the Singhalese date to be credible as the Singhalese sacred era was reckoned from it and the date matched Siamese era very well. In 1823 Julius Heinrich Klaproth presented the following list of dates of Lord Buddha's birth according to various traditions: 961 BCE according to Mongolian, 1027 BCE according to Chinese, between 1029 to 960 BCE according to Japanese, 1366 BCE according to Abul Fazl and 2009 BCE according to a Hindu work Bhāgavatāmṛta. In 1825 Wilson calculated 1332 BCE as the date of Nirvāṇa of Lord Buddha according to Kalhaṇa's Rājataraṅgiṇī.

Thus we see that there were a number of dates for the year of birth of Lord Buddha with majority of them being around or before 1000 BCE. Purāṇas give the earliest dates for the birth of Lord Buddha. As quoted above, one work Bhāgavatāmṛta gave 2009 BCE as the year of birth of Lord Buddha based on Purāṇas. This was the work that was quoted by Pandit Rādhākānta to Sir William Jones in eighteenth century:

> On my demanding written evidence, he produced a book of some authority, composed by a learned Goswami, and entitled Bhagawatamarita, or the Nectar of the Bhagawat, on which it is a metrical comment; and the couplet which he read from it deserves to be cited. After the just mentioned account of Buddha in the text, the commentator says,
>
> > 'He became visible, the-thousand-and-second-year-of-the-Cali-age being past; his body of-a-colour-

> between-white and-ruddy, with two-arms, without-hair on his head.' [2]

The dates of Lord Buddha based on Purāṇas do not match though. While Bhāgavatāmṛta gave the year of birth of Lord Buddha as 2009 BCE, Pandit Kota Venkatachelam calculated the year of birth to be 1887 BCE [3]. However, it can be safely said that the year of birth of Lord Buddha is closer to 2000 BCE according to the Purāṇas.

The currently accepted year of birth of Lord Buddha was calculated based on the identification of the Indian king Sandrokottos from Greek accounts with Chandragupta Maurya by Sir William Jones in 1793 CE [4]. Most of the modern historians place the birth of Lord Buddha in the sixth century BCE (sometime between 567-563 BCE) and his Nirvāṇa in the fifth century BCE (sometime between 487-483 BCE). Since Indian and Chinese dates are too early, modern historians have argued that Singhalese/Sri Lankan dates are the most reliable. However, what the historians have fed us as most reliable also results in a chronological dilemma that is impossible to resolve. This problem has been stated by Theodor Benfey in 1839 in the following words:

> … all Ceylonese chronicles begin their history with the year 543 B.C., the Nirvāṇa of Gautama Buddha. … we can hardly place the beginning of Chandragupta's reign earlier than 312 B.C. According to the chronology of Mahavamsa, however, Chandragupta's accession to power dates to the year 381 B.C. The difference thus amounts to 69 or 70 years. One can see from this that two types of dates – one pertaining to Indian history and

> others to the life of the Buddha – are joined in a synchronism, without matching up. [1]

Let me explain this problem further. Modern historians have calculated the date of the Lord Buddha from the date of Aśoka Maurya, whose date of coronation has been fixed at ~268 BCE, based on his identification with Devānāmpriya Priyadarśī. According to Singhalese texts the coronation of Piyadassi took place 218 years after the Nirvāṇa of the Lord Buddha and therefore the Nirvāṇa of Lord Buddha took place at ~486 BCE. This will place the year of his birth 80 years earlier at ~566 BCE. However, the same Singhalese texts that mention 218 years between the Nirvāṇa of Lord Buddha and coronation of Piyadassi are also emphatic that Nirvāṇa of Lord Buddha took place in 543 BCE. Counting from this date the coronation of Aśoka Maurya took place 218 years later in 325 BCE, which is around the time of the invasion of India by Alexander. This will make Aśoka Maurya the contemporary of Alexander instead of his grandfather Chandragupta Maurya, who must be placed 50 years earlier in 375 BCE. Chandragupta Maurya can then no longer be the contemporary of Alexander and the identification of Sandrokottos of Greek accounts with Chandragupta Maurya fails.

Modern historians are telling us that the place farthest from the birthplace of Lord Buddha has preserved the most authentic date of his birth. There is simply no reason for Singhalese texts to be more reliable than Indian, Chinese, and Nepalese texts. It is more likely that the most authentic information about the birth of Lord Buddha was preserved in a place closer to his place of birth. I would like to propose that this has indeed been the case and this information is to be found in an astronomical text called the Sumatitantra, the first book on astronomy from Nepal. The relevant verses from Sumatitantra are presented and discussed in a paper titled "Mānadeva Samvat: An Investigation into an Historical Fraud" by Kamal P. Malla [5]. We should note the title of the paper, which is symptomatic of the attitude that modern historians have towards our ancient records. The objective is not to understand what they mean but to declare as forgery whatever does not suit the accepted chronology. What is being dismissed as a historical fraud not only provides information about the date of Lord Buddha, but also provides evidence in support of the Imperial Guptas being contemporary of Alexander. In addition, it provides the identification of Emperor Śudraka, whose writing Mṛcchakaṭikam is well known, but whose identity is unknown. Sumatitantra contains the following verses:

> "jāto duryodhano rājā kalisandhyam pravarttate |
> Yudhiṣṭhiro mahārājo duryodhanastayopi vā ||
> ubhau rājau sahasre dve varṣantu sampravarttati |
> Nandarājyam śatāṣṭañchaśchandraguptastatopare ||
> rājyaṅkaroti tenāpi dvātriṃśachchādhikaṃ śatam |
> rājā Śūdrakadevaścha varṣasaptābdhi chāśvinou ||
> Śakarājā tatopaśchādvasurandhra kritantathā |
> ityate bhāṣitammahyam jnayā rājā krameṇa tu ||
> Śesā yutāścha kṛta ambarāgni 304 Śrī Mānadevābda prayujyamānā
> etāni piṇḍa kali varṣamāhuḥ ||

We can extract the following information from these verses:

> Yudhiṣṭhira and Duryodhana were present at the junction of Kali (with Dwāpara). Both of them continued for 2000 years, Nanda ruled for 800 years, Chandragupta for 132 years, Śūdraka for 247 years, Śaka king for 498 years and Mānadeva for 304 years.

The intended meaning of these verses will be obvious to those familiar with Indian tradition, but these verses will be incomprehensible to those not familiar with the tradition. Malla says the following about these verses:

> The above text has been transcribed, translated, and interpreted differently by different Nepali and foreign historians of Nepal, depending upon how, for instance, one translates the word, sampravarttate. Yet the fact remains that not a single of the figures for the six epoch eras mentioned in the Sumatitantra – (Yudhiṣṭhira 2000, Nanda 800, Chandragupta 132, Śūdraka 247, Śaka 498, and Mānadeva 304) matches with the known historical facts. … If the intention was to specify the duration of a king's reign or rule, then it is clearly a pious fabrication. [5]

Let's try to understand what these verses mean. It is quite obvious that these verses are not defining the ruling period of kings as no one lives for 2000 years. These verses are not defining how long the individual eras lasted, as the use of Śaka era is still continuing. What is being defined is the period between the eras listed in these verses and this yields the following very important information:

> The Nanda era started 2000 years after the Kali era. The Chandragupta era started 800 years after the Nanda era. The Śūdraka era started 132 years after the Chandragupta era. The Śaka era started 247 years after the Śūdraka era. The Mānadeva era started 498 years after the Śaka era. The text Sumatitantra was written in the 304th year of the Mānadeva era.

It is well established that the Kali era started in 3102 BCE. Therefore, according to these verses, the Nanda era started in 1102 BCE, the Chandragupta era started in 302 BCE, the Śudraka era started in 170 BCE, the Śaka era started in 78 CE, the Mānadeva era started in 576 CE, and the text Sumatitantra was written in 880 CE in the 304th year of the Mānadeva era. Since there was no zero BCE or zero CE and 1 CE followed 1 BCE, 247 years from 170 BCE falls in 78 CE instead of 77 CE. We should note that the starting date of the well-known Śālivāhana Śaka era is 78 CE, and this calculation exactly matches with it. This provides a solid confirmation for this interpretation. Since Nanda is separated by 800 years from Chandragupta, this Chandragupta has to belong to Imperial Guptas as Chandrgupta Maurya was close successor to Nanda. This verse then places Chandragupta of Imperial Gupta dynasty in 302 BCE making Imperial Guptas contemporary of Alexander and his successors instead of Mauryas.

The date of the Lord Buddha can be calculated from the information on the Nanda era provided by Sumatitantra as follows. We will use the following information from the Purāṇas for this purpose as given by Pargiter [6].

> Ajātaśatru will be king 25 years. Darśaka will be king 25 years. After him Udāyin will be king 33 years. That king will make as his capital on the earth Kusumpura on the south bank of the Ganges in his fourth year. Nandivardhana will be king 40 years. Mahānandin will be 43 years. … As son of Mahanandin by a śudra woman will be born a king, Mahapadma (Nanda), who will exterminate all kśatriyas. Thereafter kings will be of Śudra origin. Mahapadma will be sole monarch, bringing all under his sole away. He will be 88 years on the earth. He will uproot all kśatriyas, being urged on by prospective fortune. He will have 8 sons, of whom Sukalpa will be the first; and they will be kings in succession to Mahapadma for 12 years. A Brahman Kautilya will uproot them all; and, after they have enjoyed the earth 100 years, it will pass to the Mauryas. [6]

There are three Nandas in this list, Nandivardhana, Mahānandin, and Mahāpadma Nanda. We need to decide which one is intended in this text. To make the proper choice, we need to keep in mind that Lord Mahāvīra and Lord Buddha were contemporaries. In the previous chapter, I had provided information for dating Lord Mahāvīra's birth in 1244 BCE. To be consistent with this date, the Nanda era needs to start with the beginning of the reign of Nandivardhana. Based on this assumption, the chronology of Magadha kings is shown in Table 9.1.

Table 9.1: The chronology of Magadha kings

King	Reign in years	Proposed Chronology
Ajātaśatru	25	1185-1160 BCE
Darśaka	25	1160-1135 BCE
Udāyin	33	1135-1102 BCE
Nandivardhana	40	1102-1062 BCE
Mahānandin	43	1062-1019 BCE
Mahāpadma Nanda and Eight Nandas	100	1019-919 BCE

Lord Buddha died during eighth year of Ajātaśatru's reign [7]. Thus, the Parinirvāṇa of Lord Buddha took place in 1178 BCE, based on information presented in Table 9.1. As Lord Buddha had lived for 80 years, he lived between 1258-1178 BCE.

It is not a coincidence that the most authentic information about the year of birth of Lord Buddha and the era of Imperial Guptas is preserved in a text from Nepal. While Lord Buddha was born in present day Nepal, Chandragupta-I married a Lichchhavi princess and Lichchhavis had moved to Nepal subsequent to the rise of the Imperial Guptas. It means that the history of Nepal is also as messed up as that of India with Lichchhavis moving to Nepal around six centuries earlier than currently believed. A way out of the resulting confusion has been found by declaring genuine documents as forgery instead of re-examining the faulty chronology.

As we have seen in this chapter, the information that has come to us from our ancestors may be in a cryptic form. If we don't have the patience and attitude to understand the information, it will seem incomprehensible. We are inheritors of a unique civilization that has survived the ravages of time because it devised ways to preserve its knowledge base not only through literature but also through popular traditions. If we carefully analyze the information, we will find that the true history of India is completely different from what is accepted right now. The new dates for Lord Buddha and Lord Mahāvīra take the history of India back by about seven centuries and provide an opportunity to fix many chronological problems plaguing the ancient history of India.

Notes:

1. Dietz (1995): 39-105.
2. Jones (1788).
3. Venkatachelam (1956): 17.
4. Jones (1793).
5. Malla (2005).
6. Pargiter (1913): 69.
7. Majumdar, Pusalker, and Majumdar (2001): 37.

“The difficulty lies not so much in developing new ideas as in escaping from old ones.”
— John Maynard Keynes

10. An Alternative Timeline of Indian History

The history of India as we know it was compiled during the time India was colonized by Britishers. European scholars worked out the chronology of Indian history by identifying the connections between Indian and European historical figures. They identified two sheet anchors that firmly tie the Indian history to Greek history. Most of the ancient Indian history has been constructed by counting backward and forward from these sheet anchors as shown in Figure 10.1.

10.1 Current sheet anchors of Indian history

The first sheet anchor is the identification of Sandrokottos of the Greek accounts with Chandragupta Maurya, the founder of the Mauryan Dynasty. The second sheet anchor of Indian history is the identification of Devānāmpriya Priyadarśī of major rock edicts with Aśoka Maurya, the grandson of Chandragupta Maurya. These identifications are not on as solid grounds as the historians believe.

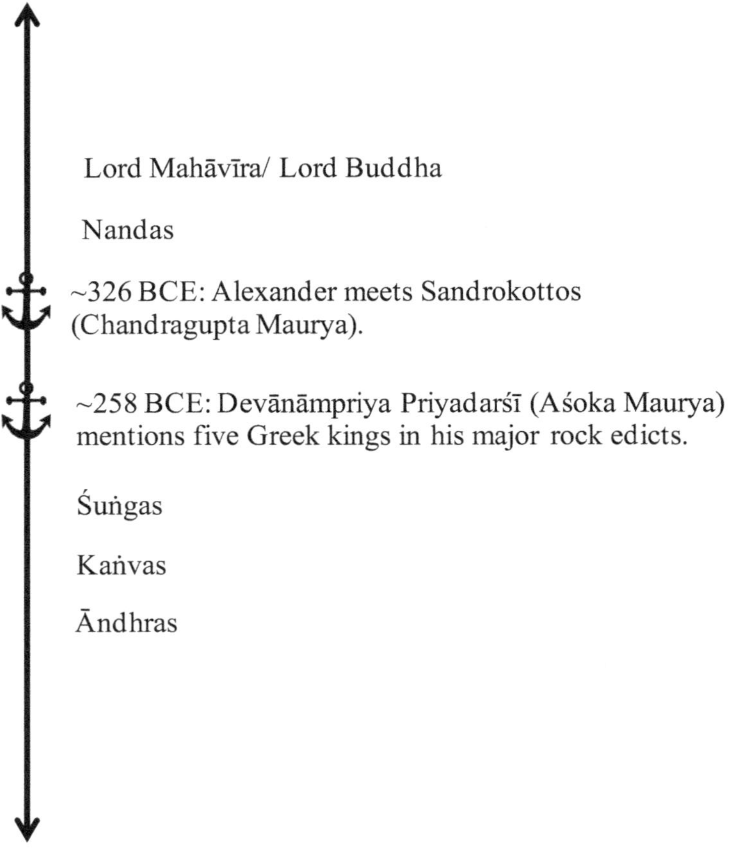

Figure 10.1: The construction of Indian chronology from accepted sheet anchors

10.2 Consequences of wrong sheet anchors

The identification of Chandragupta Maurya, the founder of the Mauryan Dynasty, with Sandrokottos of Greek accounts is based on phonetic similarity. If that is the case, then there is another namesake, Chandragupta I of the Imperial Gupta

Dynasty, who could also be the Sandrokottos of the Greek accounts. Currently, Chandragupta Maurya is considered the contemporary of Alexander the Great and Seleucus I Nicator. However, it is entirely feasible that Chandragupta I of the Imperial Gupta Dynasty was the contemporary of Alexander the Great and Seleucus I Nicator. Ancient Indian history will then be off by more than six centuries. Since the Greek accounts only give the phonetic equivalent of first name Chandragupta and not the last name Maurya, either Chandragupta Maurya or Chandragupta I of the Imperial Gupta Dynasty could be meant by them.

Let us assume for argument's sake that historians have made a mistake in identifying Sandrokottos with Chandragupta Maurya, who should really be identified with Chandragupta-I of Imperial Gupta dynasty. Chandragupta Maurya is currently assumed to have ruled during the last quarter of fourth century BCE, while Chandragupta-I is supposed to have ruled during the first half of fourth century CE. The two Chandraguptas are separated in time by roughly 650 years. This will imply that Imperial Gupta dynasty has been moved forward by over six centuries. This will have a cascading effect as shown in Figure 10.2. In this figure, a timeline has been drawn on the left side and different dynasties and important historical figures are shown on the right. The arrows qualitatively show their displacement from their actual time. Historians have been forced to misinterpret evidence and fabricate theories to support the faulty timeline resulting from the wrong identifications of the sheet anchors of Indian history. Indian history can be reconstructed by correct identifications of the sheet anchors of Indian history.

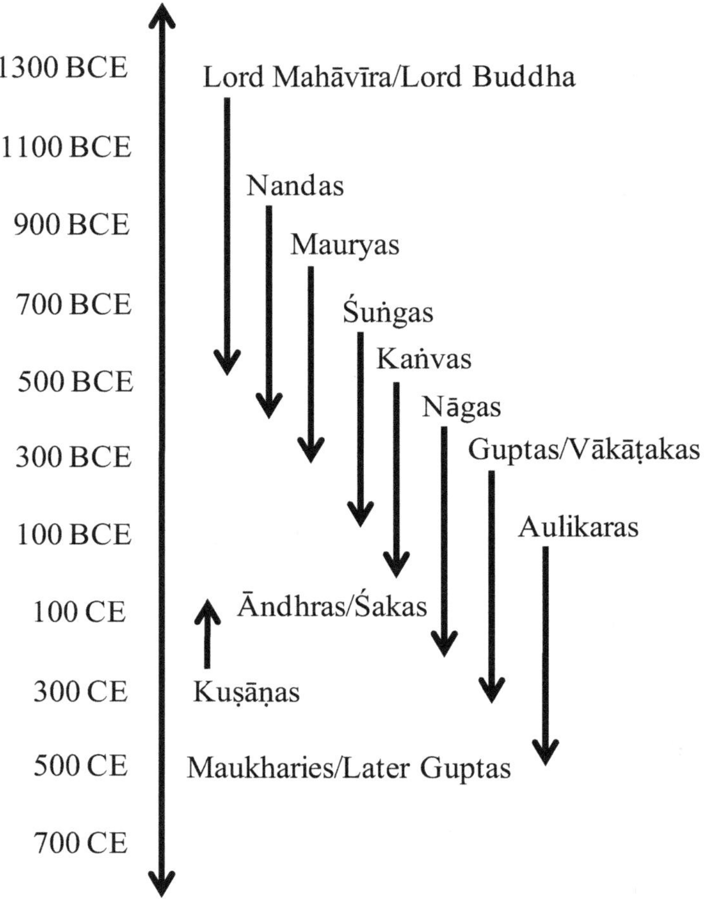

Figure 10.2: The consequences of chronology constructed from wrong sheet anchors

10.3 Alternative sheet anchors of Indian history

In my books India before Alexander: A new Chronology, India after Alexander: The age of Vikramādityas, and India after Vikramāditya: The Melting Pot, I have proposed an alternative timeline of Indian history based on alternative sheet anchors of Indian history [1-3]. These alternative sheet anchors are based on the identifications of Sandrokottos with Chandragupta-I and Devānāmpriya Priyadarśī with Kumāragupta-I, both of the Imperial Gupta dynasty, as shown in Figure 10.3.

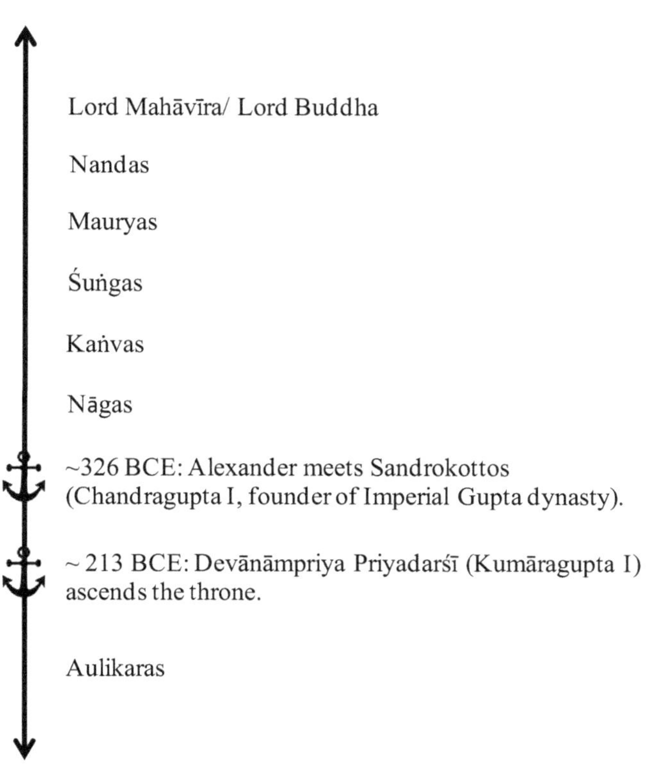

Figure 10.3: Construction of chronology based on alternate sheet anchors

Based on my work, a comparison of accepted dates of historical figures and dynasties with alternative dates is shown in Table 10.1. Most of the historical figures and dynasties have been moved forward by over six centuries. However, Kuṣāṇa dynasty has been moved backward to make room for Imperial Guptas.

Table 10.1: Accepted and alternate chronologies

	Accepted Chronology	Alternate Chronology [1-3]
Lord Mahāvīra	599-527 BCE/ 540-468 BCE	1244-1172 BCE
Lord Buddha	563-483 BCE	1258-1178 BCE
Bimbisāra (Śreṇika)	544-492 BCE	1237-1185 BCE (reigned)
Nandas	344-323 BCE	1019-919 BCE (reigned)
Chandragupta Maurya	324-300 BCE	919-895 BCE (reigned)
Bindusāra Maurya	300-273 BCE	895-870 BCE (reigned)
Aśoka Maurya	273-236 BCE	870-834 BCE (reigned)
Samprati Maurya	224-215 BCE	803-794 BCE (reigned)
Śuṅga dynasty	188-76 BCE	696-576 BCE
Kaṇva dynasty	76-31 BCE	576-531 BCE
Chandragupta I	319-50 CE	309-294 BCE (reigned)
Samudragupta	350-76 CE	294-252 BCE (reigned)
Chandragupta II	376-415 CE	252-213 BCE (reigned)
Kumāragupta I	415-447 CE	213-173 BCE (reigned)
Skandagupta	456-467 CE	172-161 BCE (reigned)
Prakāśadharmā	515 CE	130 BCE (known date)
Yaśodharmā	532 CE	113 BCE (known date)
Vallabhī dynasty	502-766 CE	144-543 CE
Kuṣāṇa dynasty	78 CE-320 CE	227-475 CE

Currently there is a huge gap in Indian history after the fall of Indus Valley civilization. There is no such gap based on the correct identification of the sheet anchors of Indian history. The textbooks of Indian history need to be revised to remove the colonial bias and present the history as it has happened.

Notes:

1. Roy (2015a).
2. Roy (2015b).
3. Roy (2015c).

Bibliography

Basham, A.L., 1951. History and doctrines of the Ājīvikas: A vanished Indian religion. Delhi, India: Motilal Banarasidass.

Burgess, E. (1860). Translation of the Surya-Siddhanta: A Text-Book of Hindu astronomy, with notes, and an appendix. Journal of the American Oriental Society, 6: 141-498.

Danino, M., 2005. Dholavira's geometry: a preliminary study. Puratattva, Vol. 35, pp. 76-84.

Danino, M., 2008. New insights into Harappan town-planning, proportions, and units, with special reference to Dholavira. Man and Environment, Vol. 33, No. 1, pp. 66-79.

Dietz, S. (1995). The Dating of the Historical Buddha in the History of Western Scholarship up to 1980. In "When Did the Buddha Live? The Controversy on the Dating of the Historical Buddha", edited by Heinz Bechert", Delhi-110007, India: Sri Satguru Publications.

Eggermont, P.H.L., 1968. The Purāṇa source of Merutuṅga's list of kings and the arrival of Śakas in India. in Papers on the Date of Kaniṣka, edited by A.L. Basham, Leiden, Netherlands: E.J. Brill.

Fleet, J. F., 1888. Corpus Inscriptionum Indicarum, Vol. III: Inscriptions of the Early Guptas, Government of India, Central Publications Branch, Calcutta, India, pages 84-88.

Gauss, C.F., 1799, Arithmetisch Geometrisches Mittel. In Werke, Volume III, Konigliche Gesellschaft der Wissenschaft, Göttingen.

Jain, K.C., 1991. Lord Mahāvīra and his times. Delhi, India: Motilal Banarasidass.

Jain, L.C., 1983. Exact Sciences from Jaina Sources, Vol. 2: Astronomy and Cosmology. Jaipur, India: Rajasthan Prakrit Bharti Sansthan.

Jain, L.C. and Jain, K.P., 1995. Certain special features of the ancient Jaina calendar. Indian Journal of History of Science. 30(2-4), pp. 103-131.

Jones, W. (1788). On the Chronology of the Hindus. Asiatick Researches or Transactions of the Society Instituted in Bengal, 2, pages 111-147.

Jones, W. (1793). The Tenth Anniversary Discourse. Asiatick Researches or Transactions of the Society Instituted in Bengal, Vol. 4, pages xii-xiv.

Joseph, G.G., 2011. The Crest of the Peacock, 3rd edition, Princeton, New Jersey, USA: Princeton University Press.

Kaye, G.R. (1924). Hindu Astronomy, Calcutta: Government of India, Central Publication Branch, page 118.

Keith, A.B. (1914). The Veda of the Black Yajus School entitled Taittiriya Sanhita. Cambridge, Massachusetts, USA: Harvard University Press.

Kuppanna Sastry, T.S., 1985. Vedāṅga Jyotiṣa of Lagadha in its Ṛk and Yajus recensions. Indian National Science Academy, New Delhi, India.

Lishk, S.S., 1987. Jaina Astronomy, Delhi, India: Vidya Sagara Publications.

Majumdar, R.C., Pusalker, A.D. and Majumdar A.K. (Editors). (2001). The History and Culture of the Indian People, Volume II: The Age of Imperial Unity. 7th Edition. Mumbai, India: Bharatiya Vidya Bhavan.

Malla, K. P. (2005). Mānadeva Samvat: An investigation into an Historical Fraud. Contributions to Nepalese Studies, 32 (1), pages 1-49.

Napier, J., 1614. The Description of the Wonderful Canon of Logarithms.

Ohashi, Y., 1994. Astronomical Instruments in Classical Siddhantas. Indian Journal of History of Science, 1994, Vol. 29, No. 2, pp. 155-313.

Pandeya, R.B., 1951. Vikramāditya of Ujjayīnī. Banaras, India: Shatadala Prakashana.

Pargiter, F. E. (1913). The Purana Text of the Dynasties of the Kali Age. London, UK: Humphrey Milford and Oxford University Press.

Pascal, B., 1653. Treatise on Arithmetical Triangle.

Pingree, D., 1973. The Mesopotamian origin of early Indian mathematical astronomy. Journal of the history of astronomy, Vol. 4, pp. 1-12.

Pingree, D. and Morrissey, P. (1989). On the identification of the “Yogatārās” of the Indian Nakṣatras, Journal for the History of Astronomy, 20.2: 99-119.

Roy, R.R.M., 2015a. India before Alexander: A New Chronology. Mississauga, Ontario, Canada: Mount Meru Publishing.

Roy, R.R.M., 2015b. India after Alexander: The Age of Vikramādityas. Mississauga, Ontario, Canada: Mount Meru Publishing.

Roy, R.R.M., 2015c. India after Vikramāditya: The Melting Pot. Mississauga, Ontario, Canada: Mount Meru Publishing.

Roy, R.R.M., 2018a. Estimation of Time from Shadow Length in Ancient Jain Astronomy, ISJS-Transactions, Vol.2, No.1, January-March, 2018, pp. 9-23.

Roy, R.R.M., 2018b. Seasonal Variation of Shadow Length in Jain Astronomy, ISJS-Transactions, Vol.2, No.2, April--June, 2018, pp. 12-25.

Roy, R.R.M., 2018c. Identification of Taxila as the Original Centre of Vedic and Jain Astronomy, ISJS-Transactions, Vol.2, No.4, October-December, 2018, pp. 1-10.

Roy, R.R.M., 2020. Zero points of Vedic Astronomy. Mississauga, Ontario, Canada: Mount Meru Publishing.

Schmidt, O. H., 1944. The Computation of the Length of Daylight in Hindu Astronomy. Isis, Vol. 35, No. 3, pp. 205-211.

Sethna, K. D., 1989. Ancient India in a New Light, Aditya Prakashana, New Delhi, India, page 499.

Sharma, S.D. and Lishk, S.S. Length of the day in Jaina astronomy. Centaurus, Vol. 22: No. 3, 1979, pp. 165-176.

Shastri, A.M., 1996. Vikrama era. Indian Journal of History of Science, Volume 31, No. 1, pages 35-65.

Sridharan, R., 2005. Mathematics in Ancient and Medieval India, in Contributions to the History of Indian Mathematics, edited by G. G. Emch, R. Sridharan and M. D. Srinivas, Gurugram, India: Hindustan Book Agency.

Srinivasan, S., 1979. Mensuration in Ancient India. Delhi, India: Ajanta Publications.

Stedman, F., 1677. Campanalogia.

Stillwell, J.C., 2010. Roads to Infinity: The Mathematics of Truth and Proof. Boca Raton, Florida, USA: CRC Press.

Thapar, R. (2003). The Penguin History of Early India: From the origins to AD 1300. New Delhi, India: Penguin Book.

Venkatachelam, K., 1953. The plot in Indian Chronology, Bharata Charitra Bhaskara, Gandhinagara/Vijayawada, India, page 30.

Venkatachelam, K. (1956). Age of Buddha, Milinda & Amtiyoka and Yugapurana. Ghandhinagara/Vijayawada, India: Bharata Charitra Bhaskara.

Vijaya, B., 1957. Jain aura Bauddha ke Darśana para Nibandha. Ghanerao, Rajasthan, India: Śrī Hita Satka Jñāna Mandira (in Hindi).

Vyāsa, R. (Editor). (1990). Saṃvat-pravarttaka Samrāṭa Vikramāditya (in Hindi). Delhi, India: Pāṇḍulipi Prakāśana.

Whitney, W.D. (1905). Atharva-Veda Saṃhitā, Second Half. Cambridge, Massachusetts, USA: Harvard University Press.

Index

Also by Mount Meru Publishing

Author: Dr. Raja Ram Mohan Roy

1. Vedic Physics: Scientific Origin of Hinduism
2. India before Alexander: A New Chronology
3. India after Alexander: The Age of Vikramādityas
4. India after Vikramāditya: The Melting Pot
5. Zero Points of Vedic Astronomy: Discovery of the Original Boundaries of Nakshatras
6. An Alternative Timeline of Indian History: From Buddha and Mahavira to Bappa Rawal

Author: Professor Subhash Kak

1. The Circle of Memory: An Autobiography
2. Matter and Mind: The Vaisheshika Sutra of Kanada
3. Arrival and Exile: Selected Poems
4. Computation in Ancient India
5. Mind and Self: Patanjali's Yoga Sutra and Modern Science
6. The Nature of Physical Reality (Third Edition)

Author: Dr. Dilip Amin

1. Interfaith Marriage: Share and Respect with Equality

Author: Professor Ramesh Rao

1. The Election that Shaped Gujarat and Narendra Modi's Rise to National Stardom

About the Author

I am a seeker in search of the true history and heritage of India. I have strong scientific background (B.Tech. in Metallurgical Engineering from Indian Institute of Technology, Kanpur and Ph.D. in Materials Science and Engineering from The Ohio State University, USA) and a deep interest in ancient Indian texts. My work on Indology spans three different fields: cosmology, astronomy, and history. My first book "Vedic Physics: Scientific Origin of Hinduism" details the cosmological framework in which the Ṛgveda, first book of humankind, is to be understood. Anyone who has read the Ṛgveda with an open mind will know that the book does not make sense if taken literally as it is full of rich symbols. Many of these symbolic and mysterious sounding passages start to make perfect sense in the light of my discovery of the Ṛgveda as a coded book of cosmology.

My in-depth work on Hindu astronomy enabled by my science background led me to realize that if great Indian astronomer Varāhmihira is placed in 6th century CE as stipulated by many Indic scholars, both western and some Indian, then that essentially means that the boundaries of sidereal Hindu and western zodiacs do not match and have a difference of about 10°. The search for the origin of this discrepancy led me to reassess the boundaries of nakṣatras and identifications of yogatārās. In my book "Zero Points of Vedic Astronomy: Discovery of the Original Boundaries of Nakshatras" I show that the original boundary of Aświnī nakṣatra is at 8° from Hamal or 10° from Revatī. This crucial discovery synchronizes the sidereal Hindu and western zodiacs.

My book "Zero Point of Jain Astronomy: The Origin of Mālava Era" addresses the important question of the origin of Mālava Era. Jain astronomy provides an important link between Vedic astronomy and classical Hindu astronomy. In my book on Jain astronomy, important features of Jain astronomy have been discussed and compared with Vedic astronomy and classical Hindu astronomy. Based on the changing position of sun in the background of stars during solstices and equinoxes, the date of the astronomical observations described in Jain texts has been estimated. It is proposed that the zero point of Jain astronomy as well as Mālava era coincides with the yogatārā of Aświnī, Hamal, being at vernal equinox in 702 BCE.

As one of the inspirations of my work on Indian astronomy stems from my desire to understand the timing of the great astronomer Varāhamihira, this harmonization of Indian and western zodiacs firmly establishes Varāhmihira in the first century BCE, consistent with the Indian tradition that places him in the court of Emperor Vikramāditya. Once again, while Indian tradition fondly pays homage to the extraordinary valour of Emperor Vikramāditya in protecting India from the invaders by still counting time from 57 BCE called Vikrama era, yet regrettably many modern historians without evidence claim that there was no Vikramāditya in first century BCE. The search for Emperor Vikramāditya, in whose memory Vikrama era has been established, led me to reexamine the very foundations of Indian history. My books "India before Alexander: A New Chronology", "India after Alexander: The Age of

Vikramādityas", "India after Vikramāditya: The Melting Pot" and "An Alternative Timeline of Indian History: From Buddha and Mahavira to Bappa Rawal" detail an alternative timeline of Indian history derived from in-depth analysis of source materials. Most of the pre-Islamic chronology is based on counting backward and forward from two sheet anchors of Indian history - the identification of Sandrokottos of Greek accounts with Chandragupta Maurya and the identification of Devanampriya Priyadarshi of major rock edicts with Ashoka Maurya. With extensive background research, in my books I show that Sandrokottos of Greek accounts should be identified with Chandragupta I of Imperial Gupta dynasty and Devanampriya Priyadarshi of major rock edicts should be identified with Kumaragupta I, the great grandson of Chandragupta I.

In my work, I take extreme care in keeping my research transparent unlike some Indic researchers who give vague references and mislead readers by presenting their interpretations as evidence. In my books I fully explain the background needed to understand the subject matter, state of current scholarship, and why my thesis differs from others. You may or may not agree with my conclusions, but I hope that my books and articles will make you question the conventional history presented as facts with dubious evidence. This unscientific and dogmatic version of the history has been propagated by many Indic historians suffering from colonial mindset. It is also my sincere hope that my work will encourage others to use science as a critical tool to evaluate and understand Indian history.

www.ingramcontent.com/pod-product-compliance
Lightning Source LLC
LaVergne TN
LVHW010919110826
845149LV00013B/2423

* 9 7 8 1 9 8 8 2 0 7 2 2 3 *